THE TWELVE COMMANDMENTS

A Prescription for Modern-Day Behavior

by

William R. Endsley, Ph.D.

The Twelve Commandments:
A Prescription for Modern-Day Behavior

ISBN: 978-0-692-82100-8

To my loved ones.

And to those who I have known during my lifetime who have given me friendship, who have displayed kindness and personal integrity, who have taught me by word and example, who have been honorable under trying circumstances, and to those who keep covenants and sacred promises, who have been genuine friends, I give my personal thanks to you. You have blessed my life many times over. And to my extended family, both those present and those who have gone forward to the next life, I am honored to be part of that family. Thanks.

Table of Contents

Goal of the Book

Trying to write a book about the Twelve Commandments as a Prescription for Modern-Day Behavior is a daunting challenge. However, not only do I feel that it has to be written now, it should have been written long ago. Privately, I have wanted to write this book for many years, but like so many other would-be writers, I just kept putting it off. But finally, here it is, written in the best way that I know how. It is thus, humbly offered to the whole world, that we might become a more godly people, especially in today's wicked world.

The main motivation for the author in writing this book, alluded to above, is the definite lack of understanding among people today of what the Ten Commandments and the Two Great Commandments are, what they mean, and what they require of each of us. Do we in today's sophisticated world really need to live by the Twelve Commandments, or have we in some way outgrown them, like so many believe we have? The answer is an unequivocal statement: *We need to live according to the Twelve Commandments today just as much as at any time in the past.* The requirement for commandment obedience has not changed due to the passage of time. In fact, because of the great wickedness within the world today, due to the fact that Satan has an ever increasing wicked population to work with, *there is an even greater need to conform our behavior in full accordance with the commandments than at any other time.* The so called cvilizations of today are not so civil because of consistent disobedience of the most basic standard of human behavior, the Twelve Commandments.

The world today is well described in the second epistle of Paul to Timothy, Chapter 3, verses 1-5:

"This know also, that in the last days perilous times shall come. For men shall be lovers of their own selves, covetous, boasters, proud, blasphemers, disobedient to parents, unthankful, unholy; Without natural affection, trucebreakers, false accusers, incontinent, fierce, despisers of those that are good; Traitors, heady, high-minded, lovers of pleasures more than lovers of God;"

In the extremely complex societies of today, we need at least one universal standard of behavior for all to live by. As history can attest, all civilized societies have had to live by various standards of behavior, or they ceased to be civilized. Through His various prophets, God has written volumes that have been collected into books like the Old Testament, the New Testament, the Torah, the Koran, the Book of Mormon and other religious books. These books have set forth behavior standards for most of the human race, and some form of the Twelve Commandments, if not all of them, are found in each.

Thus, in today's harried and confused world, where better to receive the universal standard of behavior, for all the human race, than from God, our Father in Heaven and our Creator, or from His son Jesus Christ, the Creator of the world and Savior of mankind? From either of these two wonderful sources, the standard of the Twelve Commandments will be the same, because the Father and Son's purpose and plan for the whole human race is the same. Both the Father and the Son, who are both separate and individual Gods, are united and one in this purpose, and this purpose is the eternal life and exaltation of man.

The emphasis of this book is to look at the original commandments from both the Old and New Testaments, and then illustrate and/or describe how each commandment is still alive, appropriate and applicable for today's behavior. There are real-life examples of how each commandment in today's world is so easily broken, usually because of both unfamiliarity and the lack of understanding of the commandments. There is further emphasis which will illustrate how we should live today in greater fidelity with each commandment. It is my opinion as the author, that the whole human race is still under condemnation for not living the commandments and we will eventually be judged according to how well we collectively and individually live the Twelve Commandments. This is the whole purpose of the Judgement, which will come after the 1,000 years of the millennium. Be assured, our earthly behavior will be judged.

The Judgement will determine what our reward or lack thereof, will be for the eternities. Whether we will be able to live with Heavenly Father and Jesus Christ in the eternities depends upon our worthiness and faithfulness in living the commandments. If we are unworthy, unfaithful or spiritually rebellious, we will still be resurrected to life in a kingdom which will be much better than this earth life, but we will not be able to live in the glorious Kingdom of Heavenly Father and Jesus Christ. (There will be more about this later in the book).

All twelve of the commandments are still in effect today. They have not been rescinded, or been discarded, or done away for modern-day behavior. However, Jesus Christ did rescind much of the Law of Moses with its many laws of ceremony, ritual and symbolism. The laws of carnal commandments and performances and the "Eye for eye, tooth for tooth," revengeful nature as set forth by the Law of Moses were fulfilled by the teachings, death and resurrection of Jesus Christ. However, he did not do away with, as some very erroneously think, the basic laws of the gospel, which include faith, repentance, baptism, the gift of the Holy Ghost and the original Twelve Commandments. The Savior taught them and lived them, all of them, as did the many prophets who lived with Him and those prophets who have lived since. They have all individually and collectively continued to live and teach all the commandments even in The New Testament and in the other religious books. Thus, ALL the commandments are still required of us today. It is false doctrine to teach or preach otherwise. And, it is not up to modern-day man to interpret which ones to obey and reject. The Twelve Commandments are as important today as they were when they were first given a few thousand years ago.

I believe that to live in full accordance with the Twelve Commandments, one can develop a much greater closeness to, and greater love and appreciation for, Father in Heaven and His son Jesus Christ.

There are many who might qualify to be religious experts who will study and possibly question this book. So be it, this is good. However, it is not to this so called "expert" audience that the book is necessarily written. Instead, it is written to those who do not know the scriptures well and have not lived according to the Twelve Commandments in the past. Additionally, it is written to those whose behavior at the present time is not currently in accordance with the Twelve Commandments, yet who have a basic understanding of the scriptures and commandments. To foster better understanding, this book is therefore written in a simple, easy to read and understand format with proper documentation and discussion of some often misunderstood but very important concepts.

There is one specific goal I hope is reached by every reader, and it is a most important one. It is if people become expert in their own understanding of the Twelve Commandments, then hopefully they will develop greater love for God and Jesus Christ, and develop greater obedience and demonstrate more godly behavior in keeping ALL the commandments. To this end, I have written this book.

Now, as a final thought before starting your study of this book. It needs to be pointed out that some information and thinking are similar throughout the discussions of the commandments. Although each commandment is addressed separately, there are instances where one commandment is so closely identified and tied with another commandment that there is some overlapping discussion and illustration. Thus, the reader may find similar arguments as well as similar references being used in support of the different viewpoint of another commandment. There is nothing wrong with this procedure. In fact, it is a well known factor in learning that repetition is very helpful in the retention and understanding of information. However, the reader could have some cause for confusion if it was not apparent from the beginning.

In addition, I as the author agree that I am an opinionated person. You might not initially agree with all my opinions, but do not let them get in the way of your completing the book or the workbook. However, the truths presented in both books really are, in fact, truths that I have either experienced, or learned for myself. They are *not* just my own personal opinions. Be courageous and experiment upon these written words, and then determine for yourself, through prayer and fasting, whether they are true or not.

May your reading and study be fruitful and rewarding. It is easily recognized that each of us needs to improve the way we individually behave. If everyone more carefully follows the Twelve Commandments, our collective and individual behavior will improve and therein please our Father in Heaven and His son, Jesus Christ. For when we please Them, and are obedient to Their commandments, They promise us many great things that go beyond our best imagination, in our present fallen state.

Introduction

The King James version of the Bible will be the basic reference for this book, specifically, Exodus, Chapter 20; Deuteronomy, Chapter 5; and Matthew, Chapter 22:34 through 40; Mark, Chapter 12:28 through 34; and Luke, Chapter 10:25 through 37. In addition, there will be many other specific scriptures cited.

The King James version was selected as the basic reference source because it is the most universally accepted Bible within the Christian world. It is the basic standard Bible in which all others are compared. It's beautiful prose far surpasses other Bibles of modern-day man. But, if you so desire, use your own favorite version of the Bible while reading this book.

It is my belief that if you sincerely invite the help of the Holy Ghost, He will give you sufficient understanding when scriptural passages are somewhat difficult to understand. He will also help you to know that what is written in this book is true. This procedure is certainly superior to that of depending upon some of today's various money hungry religious interpreters, giving you and I their own somewhat limited and self-serving interpretations for your monetary donations. Remember, one cannot buy his or her way into eternal life.

It should be mentioned that the reader is encouraged to read the many scriptural references from the King James version cited in this book. Much of the strength of the author's arguments, opinions and feelings supported by these scriptural references. If you don't have a King James version of the Bible, it will be helpful to obtain a copy for your study. If you want to take your study a bit farther, it is suggested that you compare all the cited references in the King James version with any of the other Bibles of today. Your study should prove to be quite interesting as well as rewarding.

The reader should be made aware that in most of the sections in this book, I have included some involved doctrinal discussions. They are meant to give more enlightenment and greater understanding of the depth, breadth and overall importance of each commandment. However, there is sufficient closure following each discussion within each section, that you will have greater knowledge of and appreciation for each specific commandment.

I make another suggestion that as you read and work with this book that you make a strong effort to pray often (at least twice daily). *Ask God, our Heavenly Father, in the name of Jesus Christ, that He help you in your efforts to be spiritually stronger and more in harmony with all the commandments.* It is further suggested that each time when you begin to study this book, sincerely pray and ask for specific understanding as to what you will read and study. (I have fasted and prayed much while writing this book and it has definitely helped me). Upon finishing each study or reading session, say a prayer of thanks and express your appreciation to your Heavenly Father and then end your prayer "...in the name of Jesus Christ." When you have done so, having faith that your prayers will be answered, you *will* receive the understanding and the strength which you will need in order to be in total harmony with all the commandments. It really can be done, and you along with many others can do it, but only if you really want to. After reading this far, you probably do have enough desire to improve your personal worthiness, and good for you for wanting to do so.

The reader should also know, that the author believes as the

Apostle Paul did when he stated in 1st Corinthians 10:12-13:

> ***"Wherefore let him that thinketh he standeth take heed lest he fall. There hath no temptation taken you but such as is common to man: but God is faithful, who will not suffer you to be tempted above that ye are able; but will with the temptation also make a way to escape, that ye may be able to bear it."***

Paul indicates that God will NOT let us be tempted by Satan, or anyone else, more than we can bear. Thus, regardless of your past behavior, it is possible for you to change for the better. And most important of all, you now have the promise, and thus greater hope, that you can make the behavioral changes because you will not be tempted beyond your ability to resist or bear.

As I wrote the above paragraph, I was reminded of all those who are now in prison for misdeeds and crimes done while on this earth. If you are one of those prisoners now reading this book, *you can* still change the "inner vessel" and become a better man or woman. You still can make restitution or undo many of the things you have done wrong. And even if you have murdered, you can stop now and never do it again; you can become a much better person. Further, you can help those you have hurt, you can reorder your life, you can become a blessing to others rather than a cursing. Through Jesus Christ, you can learn to forgive others who have "wronged" you while at the same time, you can seek forgiveness from those you have "wronged." And above all, DON'T cop-out and blame others for all your problems and your misdeeds. *Take responsibility for your life now, maybe for the first time, and do something positive with it, even if it is only changing yourself from within*. But remember, that when we change for the good from within, our outside behaviors and deeds will change also for the good.

Rely on Jesus Christ to help you change. Hope and depend upon His mercy and goodness, and yet always remember that justice is God the Father's, and that it must be satisfied someway. This is one reason why Jesus Christ is our Savior. He has, in fact, satisfied the demands of justice through His wonderful Atonement for us. We now can thus receive God's mercy, *but only when we are at least trying hard and doing the very best we possibly can to be in total compliance with Their commandments.*

Now, continue your reading that your hope in good things to come will be fully realized, because of your anticipated inner behavioral changes. May you be greatly blessed in your sincere efforts to do so.

Motivation to Become a Better Person

It is hoped that as you carefully read and study this book, utilize both prayer and fasting, and then complete the suggestions and activities in the companion workbook, when ordered from the website, www.wrmendsley.com. If you do so, many positive behavioral and spiritual changes will begin to take place within you.

It was earlier stressed in this book that the most important goal in writing it was for people of all belief systems to live in full accordance with the Twelve Commandments, and to do it with greater obedience by demonstrating more godly behavior. If the above goal can not be met by most people who read and study this book, then I as the author, have failed. However, I believe in the content and format of the book, and the suggestions and activities in the workbook. I also feel that you will, in fact, experience tremendous positive behavioral and spiritual changes if you will carefully read, study, pray and carry out the suggestions and activities as directed.

I believe that people are basically good and that most people really want to live better lives and be more in-tune with God and Jesus Christ and Their commandments. Our poor behavior is not usually a matter of premeditation. I further believe that most of our poor behavior can usually be attributed to four conditions: *1)* personal selfishness, *2)* not having enough self-control, *3)* not knowing the commandments well enough to give us that self control, and *4)* not taking enough time to think and pray in terms of conforming our behavior in accordance with the Twelve Commandments.

Due to the format in which the book is written, the above four conditions are not addressed as separate and individual topics. However, each condition is more than well covered in this book.

In each of the following chapters a brief case study will first be presented which will introduce each specific commandment. There will then be a discussion of the commandment which includes as much as possible, brief information on the setting of the commandment and possibly why the commandment was given. The book will then discuss the impact of breaking each commandment and present motivating statements and suggestions for YOU, the modern-day reader, to live with better self-control and in greater harmony with ALL the commandments. This will be done using various biblical references as well as personal experience and logic to support the discussions. Thus, you will hopefully begin to have greater knowledge to extract the meaning of each commandment as applied in today's world. This usually will lead you to positive behavioral and spiritual changes, resulting in your having greater self-control.

On the other hand, knowledge of the commandments alone is usually not enough to necessarily produce the positive behavioral and spiritual changes resulting in greater self-control. For this reason, the workbook is available for you at our website, www.wmrendsley.com.

You are encouraged to become actively involved by daily making many small behavioral changes. (You are invited to use the workbook to assist with your progress.) These small changes will help you to gain in strength and ability in keeping each commandment with greater obedience and fidelity.

In addition, you will be motivated to develop a greater sense and desire to live a more consistently faithful and righteous life.

You, as the reader, may be asking why? Because you will have acquired a significantly increased personal love and appreciation for God our Heavenly Father and His son Jesus Christ. This love and appreciation will become a great motivating force for you as you apply the principles and concepts contained in this book into your own personal behavior.

In psychology it is taught that human beings have two basic types of motivation, extrinsic and intrinsic. Extrinsic (or external) motivation is a condition wherein there are external rewards, either positive or negative, which motivate people to exhibit certain behaviors. For example, *extrinsic motivation utilizing positive reinforcement* might mean that a child or an adult will work hard for money with which to buy candy or food, or will accomplish a difficult task for praise, or will clean their room for some privileges, or will become happy when told that he or she looks nice, or will play an instrument well for applause, and perform various other tasks, such as amateur athletic feats, for the admiration or positive adoration of the fans.

On the other hand, *extrinsic motivation utilizing negative reinforcement* might mean obeying the speed limit in order to avoid getting a ticket, or staying away from a hot stove or fire to prevent oneself from getting burned, or working barely hard enough in school to avoid getting failing grades, or not beating someone up or not stealing something to prevent oneself from going to jail, and perform various other tasks to avoid receiving some unsavory or undesired type of negative reward.

I believe extrinsic or external motivation, coupled with negative reinforcement, is often the main motivator why most modern-day people live somewhat in accordance with the Twelve

Commandments. I feel this is a sad state of affairs. In other words, we obey or seem to live according to the commandments *only* to avoid, or prevent us from having to suffer from negative effects. These negative effects are usually in the form of some type of punishment, such as going to jail or even being put to death! Today, those commandments that have no punishment implemented by man, are broken all the time without any mental reservation. People have forgotten that all the original Ten Commandments were given by Jehovah to man to be obeyed. It is not appropriate for us to pick and choose to live according to only those commandments to which modern-day man has affixed a punishment. This is especially true today.

In olden times, for many hundreds of years after the original Ten Commandments were given, to disobey any of them usually meant death by stoning!

However, negative reinforcement can, in many instances, be highly motivational. But the resultant behavior is only done to avoid something distasteful or to avoid that which we do not like. It is very much a child-like type of behavior system. It is my opinion that it is far better to be motivated through the desire to receive positive reinforcement, rather than be negatively motivated in order to avoid something distasteful, like punishment. For instance, one should live the Twelve Commandments because it makes one feel good about themselves to be living in harmony with God and with one's fellowmen. It is as simple as a basic law of physics. Living in harmony with God and Jesus Christ is self-rewarding, even though sometimes you might not be living in harmony with man! And it is a superior way of living than it is for one to live the full Twelve Commandments only to avoid punishment from either God, or from His son Jesus Christ, or even from man.

On the other hand, intrinsic *(or internal)* motivation does not have any obvious external rewards such as extrinsic motivation. Intrinsic motivation is a higher form of motivation. I feel that it is a form of motivation in which only human beings are capable of developing, although there are many in this life who never experience the positive nature of it. Intrinsic or internal motivation is more difficult to establish and carry out, but once obtained and understood, it is much more powerful and longer lasting than extrinsic or external motivation. The person who is intrinsically motivated is motivated from within. There is no need for any external rewards whether they be positive or negative, for the person to be motivated. Thus, there is no need for money, praise, grades, approval, or even the threat of receiving something negative, in order to be motivated to accomplish various good things. Admittedly, I guess it is possible to be intrinsically motivated to do evil things. Satan, true to his form, can turn the most wonderful of things into evil in order to suit his gross purposes. However, this book will focus more on the good things which can result from intrinsic reinforcement.

Although the reward of Heaven might seem to be an external reward, it can also be an internal reward such as having some Heaven on Earth within your own personal life. Thus, are we supposed to live righteously just in order to receive the reward of Heaven, or to receive the greater reward of eternal life with Heavenly Father and Jesus Christ? Or are we supposed to live righteously because of our great love for Heavenly Father and Jesus Christ, coupled with our desire to be like Them and to live with Them? Or can our ultimate reward simply and appropriately encompass both aspects of motivation? Interesting questions! Although it may seem impossible to us, probably because we really know so little about eternal things and are so prone to sin, the scriptures actually do indicate that we can become like God and Jesus Christ. (See 1st John 3:1-3). Maybe as you read, study, and pray about this book, you will be better able to answer these questions for yourself. Or maybe they are questions wherein there are no right or wrong answers!

Generally speaking, it is most likely that initially, it takes an external reward to get us working towards a certain goal. In the process of working towards that goal, our motivation can change to a more mature internal motivation. Thus, we may have been initially motivated to obtain eternal life with Heavenly Father and Jesus Christ because it is such a great external reward. And there is nothing really wrong with working towards this or other wholesome external rewards. However, as we learn more about the wonderful nature and gifts of Heavenly Father and Jesus Christ, our love and appreciation will increase to a point that we will want to be like Them and eventually live with Them. Thus, our behavior can thereafter be patterned after Theirs, and our reward is knowing that we are becoming to be more like Them a little bit at a time.

We can progress to a point in our life where we really can do as Jesus would do if He were on the earth today. That should be our main intrinsic goal. Consider the latest fad bracelet which has W.W.J.D. written on it. Of course, the W.W.J.D. stands for "What Would Jesus Do?" I think it very interesting that a modern-day "fad" could possibly lead to righteous action rather than to evil deeds. Seriously, if there were many more men and women in the world today who really would always do as Jesus would do, whether they wear the bracelet or not, the world would be a significantly different and much better place. It would be a place where love, faith, hope and charity, coupled with peace, would abide. What a different place this world would be!

In the business arena, people are usually motivated through external means such as money, and this is usually measured in the *quantity* of work performed. On the other hand, internal motivation at work is usually measured in the *quality* of one's work. Measuring quality of work performed is a much more difficult task than measuring only quantity; but one who is experienced usually recognizes quality when it is observed. However, when one is not used to the presence of quality, it is actually more difficult to recognize when quality is absent. This is especially so when business owners and bosses are more often required to focus on measuring the quantity of work performed rather than focusing on measuring the quality of work performed. The resulting problems of focusing on quantity at the expense of quality, or external verses internal emphasis, are inferior products, unfulfilled and restless workers, and reduced company image.

The modern-day effort of many businesses in implementing Total Quality Management (TQM) systems is an attempt to have workers be more motivated internally towards quality management rather than be motivated through external means. Some companies have well implemented TQM well, while others have failed miserably. Those companies who have succeeded generally have satisfied employees (and customers) who are personally enough concerned about the quality of the products or services they provide, that they are willing to be very proactive to insure that the quality stays high. When companies can clearly demonstrate that poor quality negatively affects each individual worker, TQM is usually adopted universally by the workers.

A person who is more often internally motivated, performs tasks or exhibits behaviors because accomplishing the tasks or behaviors become rewarding themselves. In other words, the tasks or behaviors become self-rewarding. This is why creative people are more often internally motivated rather than externally motivated. However, not all tasks or behaviors are by themselves, internally motivational. And it should be remembered that one does not just learn automatically how to be internally motivated. It takes hard work and dedication to become so motivated.

Children usually learn motivation through external means first. As the child develops and grows older he or she learns that some of their learned behaviors become quite internally motivating and thus become self-rewarding. When one initially becomes proficient, either in accumulating knowledge, demonstrating certain behaviors or in performing specific skills, it is largely due initially to external motivation. However, if the person persists over time in gaining even greater proficiency, knowledge, behaviors or skills, he or she will likely become more internally motivated than externally motivated. The person thus gains significant self-satisfaction or obtains a large internal positive reward just by demonstrating or performing the knowledge, behavior or skill. For example, there are many artists and performers who are paid well for their performances. However, in many cases, they would continue to perform even if they were not paid well for their performance.

And the reason for this is that the knowledge, behavior or skill they possess has become self-rewarding.

Amateur athletics is a great example of internal reward systems. For example, why would any one in their right mind run a marathon? It certainly isn't for the t-shirt or the usual free dinner the night before the race. It is for the feeling of accomplishment, the feeling of self-satisfaction in finishing such a long and difficult race. I, as the author, can personally testify to this as I prepared and ran the St. George Marathon in October 1998 at the age of 56. I did it again in October of 2002 at the age of 60! I have also ridden my bike through several Century races, and have run several 10-K races, but running the marathon was a unique experience. Both times were very satisfying. I am a great fan of amateur athletics, however I feel quite differently about professional athletics, which will be addressed later.

A number of years ago the great science fiction writer Ray Bradbury stated on a live talk show in Phoenix, that he was the luckiest guy alive because he was paid for doing what he loved to do. He said that he, in fact, was paid very well for doing what he loved to do. And then he said that he probably should not say it over the radio, but that he would still write science fiction even if he were not paid for it! Ray Bradbury was intrinsically or internally motivated in writing science fiction, and he just happened to get paid well for it because he is very good at it.

We then, in the grand scheme of things, need both extrinsic (external) and intrinsic (internal) motivation to help balance our lives. However, we usually learn best in moving from external to internal motivation, and the task remains that we all need to advance to the higher level of being a more internally motivated people to do good. We need to do this rather than depend on our need for all the external motivators the world now has to offer. This is especially so for behaviors which are addressed by the Twelve Commandments. We all need to better live the commandments because high compliance is very self-rewarding, self-satisfying and brings us closer to God and Jesus Christ. Commandment keepers are greatly appreciated by God, and those who keep the commandments usually know this on an individual basis. Commandment keepers usually behave well in society.

The baseball player Cal Ripkin and the basketball player A.C. Green come to mind when the author thinks of all the highly-paid athletes who perform their skills before millions of fans. However, the difference between Mr. Ripkin and Mr. Green and so many other professional athletes, is that these two athletes were more internally motivated than most other professional athletes. Day-after-day and night-after-night they came to play their respective sports whether they were sick, injured or discouraged.

Mr. Ripkin now holds the record at 2,632 for the most consecutive games played by any other baseball player. In 1997 when this book was first written, his new record continued for over one year after the old record was broken. The old record of 2,478 games is a record that most recognized sports people said years ago, would likely never be broken! That Lou Gehrig, the original holder of the record, would always hold the record. But the record is now Mr. Ripkin's, and he continued to extend it, even into late 1998 when this book was first printed.

Mr. Green now holds the record for the most consecutive games played by any other basketball player. The old record of 906 games, held by Randy Smith, was also a record thought to be unbreakable. Mr. Green's record continues as this book was being written. Ripkin's record is several hundred more games than Green's, which is equivalent to a few more seasons, but it should be remembered that basketball is a more rigorous sport on the body than is baseball.

Mr. Ripkin and Mr. Green were initially most likely motivated externally to break their respective records due to all the fame and fortune it might bring them; but at another point in their careers, they evidently became more internally motivated beyond all the external fame and fortune. The breaking of seemingly unbreakable records is an extremely self-satisfying reward for which these two men did not receive additional money from their respective teams. Of even more significance to the author, both men appeared in their post record-breaking game interviews to be humble and unassuming men who actually seemed embarrassed by all the fame it brought them. The internal chase of their respective records was something that just seemed to develop over time, as both men attested to in interviews following their record-breaking performances.

Athletes given the physical talents from God and motivated by internal means will be the ones who break the "unbreakable" records. On the other hand, more professional athletes today who perform well enough to finally sign the "big contract" and thus receive all the "big bucks" (external motivators), will almost always immediately suffer performance declines, from which some never recover.

Some notable professional athletes have been quite audacious to the public and press while negotiating very large contracts. One of these athletes recently said, "People don't understand because the contract isn't over how much money it is. The money isn't that important." Sure, for a multi-millionaire, this is an easy thing to say. And yet the general public observes these pampered athletes complain, gripe and moan about how they are not getting treated nor paid well enough even after signing their very large contracts. Some professional athletes have even attacked their coaches and yet still think they should be allowed to play and continue to receive their outrageous salaries. To exacerbate the situation, many wealthy professional athletes fall prey to drugs, alcohol and steriods. They ultimately become a disgrace to themselves, their families and teammates.

Cal Ripkin and A.C. Green are two of those few athletes who would likely play baseball or basketball even if they did not make the "big bucks." Yet, professional athlete salaries have become so outrageous because gullible fans keep paying the escalating fees to see them play. And, financial advisors will hold their athletes out from performing their skills until the "big bucks" are obtained. Furthermore, owners keep paying the increased salaries, and will do so until the fans have had enough and quit attending the games.

There are players in the National Basketball Association who have recently said after signing big pay contracts, that their miserable public and private behavior did not matter. Because of their contracts, they were going to be well-paid regardless of their consistent display of non-exemplary behaviors on the court as well as off the court. They are thumbing their noses right in the faces of the fans who pay their big salaries, and yet their gullible fans keep coming back! It has been several years since I have paid any of my hard earned dollars to attend a professional sporting event.

It is largely due to the negative and selfish attitudes of so many professional athletes that I have elected to not attend their games.

One very famous basketball player who recently retired, admitted in an interview that he was no role model and that people should not use him as such. He just wanted to play basketball, live the life of a wealthy person, fight and spit on people, and have nobody bother him about being a bad influence on children. I guess one has to respect him for his honesty, but somewhere along the line, he forgot that highly-paid successful professional athletes are always going to be role models to children, whether they like it or not. It comes with the territory and professional athletes should be prepared for it!

So it is in the game of life, for there are many who never graduate from their over-emphasis on external rewards, especially money. It is maybe unfortunate to professional sports that I use professional athletes for especially my bad examples. However, they are the ones most visible to both the public and press. In addition, there have been several recent examples of selfishness and greed displayed by privileged corporate executives of large companies; so professional athletes are not the only poor examples. But thankfully, I know there are also many professional athletes and business people today who, from their large salaries, have quietly set up organizations to help disadvantaged and underprivileged youth as well as battered women. In so doing, they are doing what the author thinks the Savior would want them to do. *I strongly encourage more professional athletes and corporate executives with high salaries to do similar things, and I might suggest that these activities not just be limited to underprivileged youth and battered women.*

I invite and I challenge, all professional athletes and corporate executives to further invest considerable time, effort, prayer and some self-introspection in determining what Jesus would have you do with your fortune and fame. There are many professional athletes and corporate executives, even many who have retired from their respective sports and work, who continue to involve themselves by quietly helping many people less fortunate than themselves. These are great examples of how wonderfully self-rewarding that positive internal rewards are. However, if you are not like the above good examples either active or retired, you are still encouraged to read this book and search the scriptures. Then make your own determination as to what is promised to those who are wealthy, selfish, stingy, foul-tempered, unforgiving and downright nasty. You hopefully will decide to make a personal but quietly positive difference to those who have helped you along the way. Be responsive to those who don't have a chance to be as fortunate as you, to the sick, to underprivileged children, to the elderly and to the down-trodden.

Of course, the same admonition and invitation above is given by the author to all people who have excess means. Those who have millions and billions are invited to outdo yourselves in doing good with your excess wealth. You really can not take wealth with you when you die. *But you can take your goodness, your charity and your record of blessing others with your donated time and means.* There are so many people who suffer because they "have not." If you know of any of those who "have not," don't you let them go without! Do something about it and do it quietly!

Consider the wealthy Mrs. Joan Kroc, wife of the McDonald's Hamburger chain founder, Ray Kroc. She secretly donated $2,000 to EVERY flood victim of the 1996 spring floods in the midwest who applied for help. With almost no preconditions other than being a true flood victim, she gave away several million dollars directly helping those suffering people who needed help immediately. The only way she was discovered to be the secret donor was from someone identifying the tail number on her private plane as it flew away from an inspection Mrs. Kroc had made of the floods. She is setting a good example for other wealthy people to follow. Mrs. Kroc more recently donated one billion dollars to the salvation Army. Wow!

Mr. John Huntsman, one of the wealthiest men in the country is not so much pleased that he is so wealthy, but that he is listed among the top Americans in donations to a variety of worthy causes. His selective donations to education, medicine and to senior citizen causes have helped improve the lives of thousands. His "bottom line" is to always be found helping or providing for others. He is also setting a good example for other wealthy people to follow.

Mr. Hyrum Smith and his wife Gail, creators of the Franklin Day Planner, have both provided generous gifts to the fine arts to the tune of several million dollars for founding, building, and administration. Their dollars have enriched and uplifted the lives of many citizens and world-wide visitors. Prior to their financial efforts and leadership, grand-scale and first class theatrical presentations in two western state locations were few and far between.

Mr. Ted Turner's recent donation of one billion dollars to the United Nations, although somewhat controversial, is a wonderful gift to the whole world. He is also setting a good example for other wealthy people to follow, and has even verbally challenged them to do so. I further his challenge, but don't make such a big deal about it. Do it quietly. Do not do acts of charity for the plaudits of men and women. Do them quietly without fanfare, to please God and Jesus Christ, and in so doing you will be greatly blessed.

There are also many foundations who have been set up by wealthy people, not just for tax purposes, but for the blessing of others. Americans have the rare distinction, among many, of being the most giving of any people.

Being externally motivated in accumulating great wealth isn't necessarily bad, it is what ultimately is done with the wealth that is important. There are few people in this world who can righteously handle great wealth, especially those who have had it thrust upon them. Even with the wonderful gifts that wealthy people give to worthy causes, and these few mentioned above consider the Savior's teaching of the widow's mite in Mark 12:41-44, and in Luke 21:1-4:

"And Jesus sat over against the treasury, and beheld how the people cast money into the treasury: and many that were rich cast in much. And there came a certain poor widow, and she threw in two mites, which makes a farthing. And he called unto him his disciples, and saith unto them, Verily I say unto you, That this poor widow hath cast more in, than all they which cast into the treasury: For all they did cast in of their abundance; but she of her want did cast in all that she had, even all her living."

The great American philanthropists over the ages, and there have been many of them, are good examples of people being initially externally motivated only to later become more internally motivated. (This is more true of people who have earned their own wealth rather than inheriting their wealth). The giving away of wonderful gifts in either saving or enriching the lives of others can be highly motivational, especially when done in secret. It is to be strongly encouraged by those who have the wealth to be generous and giving to those individuals or worthwhile groups who need your help, sustenance and support. If you are one of those wealthy persons and don't give generously to worthy causes, then you might be like the man who came to Jesus and asked Him, "Good Master, what good thing shall I do, that I may have eternal life?" Although evidently he was a very good, moral and principled man, he was also very rich. And the scriptures indicate that probably because of all his riches when asked to give them away and follow Christ, he could not or would not, and thus probably lost out on eternal life with God and Jesus Christ. Also remember that Jesus Christ taught, "It is easier for a camel to go through the eye of a needle, than for a rich man to enter into the kingdom of God." (see Matthew 19:16-26).

All people, especially the wealthy, need to read the parable of the sheep and the goats as found in Matthew 25:31-46.

"When the Son of man shall come in his glory, and all the holy angels with him, then shall he sit upon the throne of his glory: And before him shall be gathered all nations: and he shall separate them one from another, as a shepherd divideth his sheep from the goats: And he shall set the sheep on his right hand, but the goats on the left. Then shall the King say unto them on his

right hand, Come, ye blessed of my Father, inherit the kingdom prepared for you from the foundation of the world: For I was an hungered, and ye gave me meat: I was thirsty, and ye gave me drink: I was a stranger, and ye took me in: Naked, and ye clothed me: I was in prison, and ye came unto me. Then shall the righteous answer him, saying, Lord, when saw we thee an hungered, and fed thee? or thirsty, and gave thee drink? When saw we thee a stranger, and took thee in? or naked, and clothed thee? Or when saw we thee sick, or in prison, and came unto thee? And the King shall answer and say unto them, Verily I say unto you, Inasmuch as ye have done it unto one of the least of these my brethren, ye have done it unto me. Then shall he say unto them on the left hand, Depart from me, ye cursed, into everlasting fire, prepared for the devil and his angels: For I was an hungered, and ye gave me no meat: I was thirsty, and ye gave me no drink: I was a stranger, and ye took me not in: naked, and ye clothed me not: sick, and in prison, and ye visited me not. Then shall they also answer him, saying, Lord, when saw we thee an hungered, or athirst, or a stranger, or naked, or sick, or in prison, and did not minister unto thee? Then shall he answer them saying, Verily I say unto you, Inasmuch as ye did it not to one of the least of these, ye did it not to me. And these shall go away into everlasting punishment: but the righteous into life eternal."

(Underlining added by the author for emphasis).

From that great parable, as taught by Jesus Christ in Matthew, hopefully, you can turn your external world of money, wealth and selfishness into something much more constructive and helpful to others, before it is too late! *Even those without great wealth should also do what you can to help others. There is no better scale of measurement of our personal goodness than the good things you quietly do for others!* Your own life will also be greatly enriched by your quiet good deeds and it will be well for you at the Judgement.

The point of all the discussion above is to emphasize to you that although you may presently be new in your understanding and in your living of the Twelve Commandments, you may have to start out first with basic extrinsic or external methods of motivation; for example, rewarding yourself with some small thing for perfect obedience to one of the commandments. As you progress, the reward for perfect obedience over time will become very intrinsically or internally motivating.

I, the author, have personally used this method with my own children. When our five children, especially my three sons, became old enough to attend special church meetings, they initially did not want to go. I told them that after each two-hour meeting we would get some ice cream, and that they could choose whatever flavor and topping they wanted. As I kept my promise, this procedure worked well until, and as they matured, the meetings themselves became important to them. Excellent speakers discussed topics concerning their future, their happiness, their problems, their challenges, and even their dreams. Thus, the meetings via the good speakers and pertinent topics, became the motivating force for the attendance of my three sons, rather than the ice cream. I now have little worry as to whether they will continue to attend those meetings as they grow into adulthood. We still however, go out for ice cream!

As you, the reader, again, become more knowledgeable concerning external and internal motivation, you can progress to the higher levels of internal motivation as the time, place and situation dictates. *You can and will make good progress if you try hard to be more obedient to each commandment as you learn and implement them into your life. Also, if you again apply the suggestions and activities as directed, fast and pray in the name of Jesus Christ, work hard and be consistent, you will be successful.* And thus, you will eventually become much more internally motivated, especially if you did not start out that way. And as your knowledge and understanding increase, your love and appreciation for God and His son Jesus Christ will increase. As you experience these things, your love and appreciation will become the internal motivation for you to live a better and more pure life. When you arrive at this higher behavioral condition, you will be well on your way to becoming worthy of eventually receiving all that the Father has prepared for you. All that He has prepared for you is beyond all of our wildest expectations, as you will hopefully come to understand as you progress through this book.

Now, as you get ready to go forward and begin reading and studying each commandment, do so with confidence. Read all the references, study hard and work carefully through the suggestions and activities in the workbook for each commandment and earnestly fast and pray in the name of Jesus Christ. You now have the blueprint for your own personal success. Your personal reward will be great. *It will be more than well worth any effort that you might put forth.* Best wishes for your success.

1st Commandment

"Thou shalt have no other gods before me" Exodus 20:3

Karl had been the best worker in the plant. However, lately his co-workers had noticed a distinct moodiness in Karl, especially in the morning. Some had even smelled alcohol when Karl walked by them. After several weeks of decreased work performance and increased use of alcohol, one morning Karl took a swing at his supervisor and knocked him over a work bench. Karl left the plant before anyone could stop him. He was later found by one of his friends in a drunken stupor in one of the local bars. Karl was taken home by the friend.

An article in the local newspaper, published on the following day, indicated that an hour after Karl had been taken home, he beat his wife severely and then attempted suicide before he passed out from too much alcohol. Neighbors had called the police because of all the loud arguing and fighting going on in Karl's house. As the police were approaching the home, Karl unsuccessfully tried to take his own life.

Alcohol has become Karl's God. Regardless of the reason, alcohol has become more important than anything else in Karl's life. In his quest for alcohol, Karl has lost a lot. He has lost his dignity, his self-respect, and the love of his family. If he continues on his present course, he could lose everything, including his own life, or even the life of someone else.

Do you, like Karl, have any other "gods" which come before or have become more important to you than God our Father or His son Jesus Christ? How about money, alcohol, drugs, sex, fame, self-pride, "babes" or "hunks," cars, homes, jewelry, paintings, property, acclaim, position, or anything else? If you do have any of the above or other gods, you need to keep reading.

Just what does it mean to actually have other gods before God, our Heavenly Father, or gods before Jesus Christ, our Savior and God Jehovah of the Old Testament? It means that we need to put both the Father and His son Jesus Christ *first* in all that we do. We must worship Them first and only Them. We do not put the virgin Mary, as is being done so often today, nor any of the saints, nor any statue or anything of this world or anybody else first before God the Father and Jesus Christ. We must put Them *first* and then diligently do what They have commanded us to do. It is only then that we can give attention to our own personal life, our families, our jobs, our careers, our problems, our property or even our poverty. The poor man is not any more exempt from living this commandment, and all the other commandments, than is the rich man.

The children of Israel had great problems with this commandment. They would often stray from their belief in Jehovah and ended up worshiping a variety of things and other false gods, thus disobeying the First Commandment. They also suffered greatly because of this. (Might there be a parallel happening awaiting America?) Their exodus from Egypt and their wondering around in the desert for 40 years could have been significantly eased had they kept firm in their belief in and worship of Jehovah. In addition, their eventual rejection of Jehovah and His commandments would lead to the ten tribes' destruction and subsequent scattering across the earth. These people are collectively known as the lost Ten Tribes of Israel. However, they will not always be lost. The scriptures foretell of their being gathered in the last days. (see Jeremiah, chapters 3, 16, 23 and 31, and Zechariah, chapters 2, 7 and 10). I believe these "last days" are upon us today. I personally think this great gathering to Israel and to America is now going on and will yet manifest itself in a most wonderful way some day in the future. Their coming forth from oblivion will likely overshadow in greatness many of the great religious events in the Old Testament, including the wondrous crossing of the Red Sea by the children of Israel.

Like the children of Israel of old, the modern-day rejection of God as our only God and our only Creator is presently bringing us the serious consequences of disobedience. We have as a world society strayed very far from biblical truths and standards of behavior. Look at all the gross wickedness today that we experience on a daily basis. We have even become so accustomed to it that as it goes on literally in front of our eyes, we are not even shocked by it and furthermore, we do nothing about it!

Generally speaking, people have forgotten God in their everyday lives. The murders, the abortions, the molestation, the immorality, the rape and abuse of both adults and children, the wicked and unnatural gay and lesbian movement, the greediness, the pride, the idolitry, the lying, the gross coveting, the cheating, the stealing, the lack of love of family and country are rampant. This is not only true in this country but on a world-wide basis as well. Without allegiance, dedication and service to God in this life, we are doomed to fail in even the basics of life We really have become ripe for destruction.

In the Book of Numbers, chapter 25, Moses instructed in verse 5, that the judges of Israel were to slay everyone who had embraced and worshipped the Moabite god of nature, Ball-peor. For any of the children of Israel, to worship anything or anyone other than Jehovah in the old testament, usually would suffer the pains of death. Today, there is no such punishment for breaking the First, and probably the most important Commandment of the original Ten Commandments. Today, people outright state and seriously believe there is no God. Can you imagine that?

The wonderful attribute of faith seems to have all but disappeared from many in this world. Paul describes faith as to have hope in things which are not seen, but which are true (see Hebrews 11:1). It is this faith that must be centered in Jesus Christ in order for salvation and eternal life to be the received. We should all carefully remember, that we all were created for a purpose, and that purpose is to gain eternal life through Jesus Christ (see John 17:3). Salvation and eternal life with Heavenly Father and Jesus Christ is not a free gift, as many would want you to believe. It must be faithfully earned. The free gift that the Savior provided, which is amply discussed in the new Testament and is often stated as salvation, is obtained from His wonderful Resurrection. That consists of life eternal with a resurrected body, but not necessarily living in Their presence. Everyone who has lived in this world will receive this type of salvation (being resurrected). But in obtaining eternal life with Heavenly Father and Jesus Christ, we must thoroughly demonstrate our obedience to God by repenting often and by carefully living an *increasingly more righteous life.* We must endure to the end of our life and then return honorably from this earth that we might hopefully inherit that eternal life with Heavenly Father and Jesus Christ. Of course, this is not an easy task and it will take a lifetime of learning, praying, repenting, working hard, changing our sinful nature, and getting much better in our obedience to all the commandments.

The attainment of eternal life with Heavenly Father and Jesus Christ requires more than just beliefs contrary to what many ill informed Christians believe. I wish it were just that easy, but much more is required. (There will be more discussion on this important subject later in this book).

How then specifically does the First commandment apply to us today and what can you do if you are struggling to fully obey the First Commandment? Many struggle with this commandment because we get so caught up in the world we live in. We get side tracked with all our responsibilities and requirements, that we sometimes give allegiance to things other than to God. We must be very careful with this commandment. If we read the scriptures regularly and have our personal prayers on a daily basis, this will help to center us and to keep us on track.

Note: For a final reminder, your are encouraged to obtain the workbook. Therein are specific suggestions and instructions pertaining to each commandment which will be very informative and helpful to you. See our website to obtain a copy of the workbook.

2nd Commandment

"Thou shalt not make unto thee any graven image, or any likeness of any thing that is in heaven above, or that is in the earth beneath, or that is in the water under the earth: Thou shalt not bow down thyself to them, nor serve them: for I the LORD thy God am a jealous God, visiting the iniquity of the fathers upon the children unto the third generations of them that hate me; And showing mercy unto thousands of them that love me, and keep my commandments." Exodus 20:4-6

Steve was an energetic and bright young man with a goal to become a millionaire before he was 35 years old. He had a beautiful young wife with two precious little children, and they all participated in church activities. They even paid a 10% tithing to their church, gave to charities and said their daily prayers. Steve also had a good, well-paying job as a stock broker and they all lived together in a beautiful home in an upscale area of town. But he wasn't satisfied. He felt he needed to make more money, much more money, in order to make his goal.

Steve's attention to his duties as a husband and father diminished as he became more involved in various multi-level marketing plans, risk-bond management programs, no-money-down real estate transactions and other get-rich-quick schemes. As his financial empire blossomed, his home and church life deteriorated. After several attempts to save the marriage, the young wife filed for divorce. Sure, Steve was rich as to the things of the world, but the most precious things, his wife and family and church, were not his anymore. He had willingly and knowingly lost them all. He did not even say his prayers anymore.

Did Steve have a problem with the Second Commandment? He surely did! He came to love money, or at least that which money could buy, or maybe he came to love just the thrill of making money more than he loved God and his own family. He lost sight of the most precious things in life. I believe that this is the reason that God gave us the Second Commandment, so we can keep the most important priorities well in focus. That we can focus on eternal things rather than in just accumulating the temporary things of this world. Idolitry is a sin that God really dislikes.

The Second Commandment is somewhat unusual in that it seems to be a continuance of the First Commandment of "Thou shalt have no other gods before me." We must remember that shortly after receiving the Ten Commandments, the Twelve Tribes of Israel began to worship a newly-molted golden calf, fashioned with a graving tool by Aaron, the brother of Moses (see Exodus Chapter 32). This was a great sin before the Lord, and about 3,000 men died by the swords of the Levites as a direct consequence. The sin of having other objects or things (other gods) before God our Father in Heaven, and His son Jesus Christ or the Jehovah of the Old Testament, was a serious sin then and it is still a serious sin today, even though most people do not recognize it.

In Deuteronomy 4:23-28, there is a vivid description of what was to happen to Ten of the Twelve Tribes of Israel for breaking the Second Commandment, and this was probably done in conjunction with breaking the First Commandment. Israel was scattered among the heathen nations of the earth, to then worship the gods of man. It will only be in the present latter days, and the author believes it has already begun, that the lost Ten Tribes of Israel will begin to be found, reclaimed, gathered and then have access to the blessings that father Jacob originally gave them (see Genesis Chapter 49).

The sin of breaking the Second Commandment was indeed a serious one, as the lost Ten Tribes of Israel can attest. If one can remember their Old Testament teachings (see I Kings 11), King Solomon's wives turned his heart to worship false gods and also because of the heavy taxes imposed by both King Solomon and his son Rehoboam, the Twelve Tribes of Israel were divided into two kingdoms. Ten of the tribes became the northern kingdom, and the two tribes of Judah and Benjamin became the southern kingdom. The northern kingdom went into apostasy and thus, broke the First and Second Commandments and probably all the other commandments, and began adopting the practices of Baalism. This was done even though the prophets of Elijah and Amos preached mightily among the people. Following a period of 200 years and 19 kings, the northern kingdom was "carried away" by the Assyrians, and thus became known as the "lost Ten Tribes of Israel."

The sin of breaking the Second Commandment seems to be more easily broken today with all of our many "things" of today to worship, other than God. Yet remember, that we are under just as much condemnation today when we break the Second Commandment as were the Twelve Tribes of Israel, our forefathers, many years ago.

The prophesies of the return of the lost Ten Tribes indicate that their return might be a more spectacular event than the event of the children of Israel coming out of Egypt during the time of Moses (see Isaiah 11:10-16 and Jeremiah 3:18, 16:14-21).

In addition to the general statement of the Second Commandment itself, as provided above, we are therein taught several things. God first tells us very comprehensively that we should not make or have anything graven (something carved, shaped or sculptured) or made images (pictures, or statues, or medallions, or beads, or yes, even crosses), that we pray to or worship. Also, we are taught that we should not bow down to any of these things, nor should we serve them in any way.

As the author, I believe that God the Father is a resurrected being just like His son Jesus Christ is, for Jesus Christ tells us many times in the New Testament that if someone saw Him, then that person has in essence seen the Father as well. They are alike in looks as well as in what They are trying to accomplish with all mankind, as children of God (see John 14:9-14, 5:25-38). They are united in all that they do. This is why They are alike. They are together in unity and purpose. But, They do this as separate individuals, not as two or three magic entities in one, as so many falsely believe. And, why would the Father not be resurrected, as Jesus Christ was? Since They are so alike and yet are separate beings, we thus must worship Them as the resurrected and perfect beings that They are. *We should not worship anyone or anything else!*

Jesus Christ would likely counsel us today, as He did in the New Testament, to worship only God, our Father in Heaven. *And that is what we are to do.* But it is also very appropriate to give great reverence, thanks and obedience to what Jesus Christ has taught us in the Old Testament as Jehovah, in the New Testament as Jesus Christ and in other books as the Messiah, Redeemer, and Savior.

The relationship of God the Father and Jesus Christ to each other *and* to man can sometimes be confusing. This is due to much being lost or not correctly translated in the various translations of the Bible. However, when the reader begins to fully understand who God our Father in Heaven really is, and who His son Jesus Christ is, then we can unravel the confusion. God the Father is, in fact, the Master Planner, the Master Designer, the Great Creator, the Great God of all the universe, the God of Gods and of Lords, the one we pray to and the one we generally refer to when we speak of God. He is the one that Jesus Christ prayed to, the spiritual and literal Father of Jesus Christ, and the spiritual Father of all mankind (see 1st Corinthians 8:5-6).

On the other hand, God the Father is not the God "I AM" of the Old Testament, who made Himself known to Moses (see Exodus 3:14-15). He also is not the unspoken Hebrew God of Yahveh, or Jahveh, or even the modern-day equivalent of Jehovah (see John 8:28, 56-58). (It should be noted that the name and/ or title of "I AM" from Greek, as used in the verses in John, is identical to the Septuagint usage in Exodus 3:14 translated in English as Jehovah). I AM signifies "The Self-existent One," "The Eternal," and "The First and the Last." Further, in John 8:28, Jesus also announces His name to be "I am," but the King James translators added the italics "...*he*, and *that*" to the original Hebrew or Greek text so it supposedly might make more sense in English. They also changed "I AM" from the Old Testament to "I am" in John. But as the reader can determine from the evident intent of the Savior, "I AM" and "I am" should be the same, and they both constitute but one of the many names of Jesus Christ. The translators did similar in John 4:26, 8:24, 13:19 and 18:5-8, where again the italics "*he*" is added. However, all they did was cause confusion because the inconsistent translators did not use italics in John 8:58 where the Savior *clearly and correctly* states that He is the God, I AM.

The Jews forbade even the utterance of the sacred name I AM, yet in the verses in John, Jesus Christ rightfully spoke and claimed the name as His own. In response, the Jews seized stones to kill Him, but His time was not yet, and he somehow slipped through the crowd and departed the temple. There are many Christians today who erroneously think as the Jews did of old on this very issue.

The clear declaration by Jesus Christ in the verses in John unequivocally state His Godship. He was the Great God of Abraham, Issac, Jacob, and yes, even of Moses. Jesus Christ was the Great I AM and Jehovah of the Old Testament. Jesus Christ is also the Son, both the spiritual and literal Son of God the Father. Jesus Christ works with and under the direction of the Father, as we can learn especially throughout the book of John in the New Testament, (see Genesis 1:26 and John chapters 5, 8, 10, 12 and 14). He is also our older spiritual brother. We were with Him, as part of all Heavenly Father's spiritual children, in the pre-earth life before this world was created (see Numbers 16:22, 27:16, Ecclesiastes 12:7 and Hebrews 12:9).

Actually, many of the things that the scriptures indicate were accomplished by God were really done by the Lord Jesus Christ, as Jehovah. In Genesis 1:1, where "God created the heaven and the earth," we know that it was really Jesus Christ who was the creator, under the direction of the Father (see John 1:1-18. See also John 14:31). The Apostle Paul also had the same understanding that God (the Father) created all things by Jesus Christ when he wrote in Ephesians 3:9:

"And to make all men see what is the fellowship of the mystery, which from the beginning of the world has been hid in God, who created all things by Jesus Christ."

It should also be noted at this point that the Holy Ghost is like unto God, but He is a personage of spirit. He is not presently a resurrected being, having flesh and bones such as have the Father and Jesus Christ, who are resurrected beings. However, as a spirit, the Holy Ghost can physically manifest Himself in many places and many times at once, and He can also dwell in us and testify to our own spirits, whereas the Father and Jesus Christ can individually be in only one place at a time (see Acts 6:3, and 1st Corinthians 6:19), although their influence is everywhere throughout the cosmos.

The Holy Ghost is also referred to as the Comforter, the Holy Spirit, the Spirit of God, the Spirit, and the Spirit of the Lord. The Holy Ghost has great power (see John 14:26, Romans 15:13).

The Holy Ghost is the third member of the Godhead. He has manifest Himself in every dispensation of the gospel of Jesus Christ since the very beginning with Adam and Eve. *The main mission of the Holy Ghost is to testify that Jesus Christ is the Son of God, and that His teachings are true, and that Jesus Christ is the Savior of the world,* (see John 7:39, 14:26, Acts 5:32, 1st Corinthians 2:10-16 and 12:3). Without this knowledge given by the power of the Holy Ghost, Simon Peter could not have responded to the Savior's question and uttered the statement in Matthew 16:16 that, "Thou art the Christ, the Son of the living God.", (see Matthew 16:13-20). The Apostle Paul states in 1st Corinthians 12:3:

"Wherefore I give you to understand, that no man speaking by the Spirit of God calleth Jesus accursed: and that no man can say that Jesus is the Lord, but by the Holy Ghost."

The Holy Ghost has the power to convince people to become baptized and accept the gospel of Jesus Christ. However, there is also the gift of the Holy Ghost, which is the right to actual companionship of the Holy Ghost when one is truly living worthily. The gift of the Holy Ghost from Heavenly Father is second in importance to mankind only after the gift of Jesus Christ. One must first have manifest in his or her life the actual power of the Holy Ghost, through His testimony of Jesus Christ, and then become baptized and accept wholeheartedly the gospel of Jesus Christ (see Matthew 3:11, John 3:5). This must be done BEFORE the gift of the Holy Ghost can be bestowed. The saints in Corinth which Paul preached to, were baptized members of the church and thus already had the gift of the Holy Ghost, as stated in 1st Corinthians 6:19. This is why he could say "What? Know ye not that your body is the temple of the Holy Ghost which is in you, which ye have of God, and ye are not your own?"

The gift of the Holy Ghost is a supreme gift that God has given to us here on earth, but it is a gift that we have to earn. The gift of the Holy Ghost is obtained only after "proper and authorized" full emersion baptism, and is conferred on the worthy one by the laying of hands by one or more who have the proper authority to confer this gift (see Acts 2:38 and 10:37-38,44-48). In Acts 8:9-25, Simon was rebuked by Peter for his offering money in wanting the authority and power to bestow the gift of the Holy Ghost (see also John 14:15-18).

I have personally received this wonderful "gift," and it has enriched my life as only one other gift could possibly do. Again, that other gift being the gift of Jesus Christ to the world. The gift of the Holy Ghost has literally saved me from death on more than one occasion. For example, in Oakland, California. on our wedding day in September of 1970 with my first wife Marsha, who passed away in November of 1995, I had to move her things into my apartment. While happily driving my empty truck over to her apartment, and as I inattentively approached a particularly dangerous intersection, I was cautioned by a small voice in my head to slow down. Then being on alert as I slowed down, a car seemingly came out of nowhere at high speed to run the red light at the intersection. Had I not listened and heeded that small voice, I would most likely have been killed because the car would have hit me directly on the driver's side.

The companionship of the Holy Ghost has also sustained me when things were tough and has also been the force that has given me insight and knowledge that I could not get from any other source. The inspiration to write this book actually came from the Holy Ghost

The gift of the Holy Ghost can also act in cleansing and purifying one before sanctification from all sin. This is the reason the gift is often spoken of as "fire," (see Matthew 3:11). On the day of Pentecost in Acts 2, the gift of the Holy Ghost came upon the Twelve Apostles. Without this great event taking place in the lives of these men, they would not have been ready and prepared for their ministries to the world.

In the Second Commandment, God also tells us that He is a "jealous God." Isn't that interesting, that God can be jealous? In fact, He tells us in the commandment above that He becomes jealous when we worship something or anything other than Himself. For instance, say that you worship a golden calf, a statue, money, sex, tobacco, alcohol, drugs, cars, the virgin Mary, your girlfriend, your boyfriend, your large estate, your poverty, etc. Could God be really upset with you if you did really worship any of these things, or worship many other things which were not mentioned?

Worship is defined in Webster's New World Dictionary, 1996 edition, as an "extreme love or intense devotion or admiration of any kind." Are you now in trouble with God? You just might be! And believe me, you have lots and lots of company.

Reread the commandment above, to see what God says to you if you do make Him jealous. He will visit you and your children, and their children, and their children by "visiting the iniquity of the fathers upon the children unto the third generation of them that hate me;..." Wow, even our children, grand children and great grand children can suffer because of our breaking the Second Commandment! This is especially so if our breaking the commandment is knowingly and willfully done, and probably done in conjunction with breaking other commandments.

But, this doesn't seem fair, does it? On the other hand, it is more likely that we humans don't understand the ways of God. We don't understand how upsetting it must be when we turn away from God and do not acknowledge all that He has done for us and all that He wants to do for us and to give us. It is probably even more upsetting when we reject Him as our own creator and eternal Father, and/or reject Jesus Christ as our personal Savior, and Savior of all mankind. Again, idolitry is a very serious sin.

If we knowingly and willingly break the Second Commandment, we really do evidence that we actually hate God. We do this by our making Him jealous, as He states in the commandment. On the other hand, if we knowingly and willingly keep the Second Commandment, we evidence that we love God. We grow in personal fidelity and purity, and thus further evidence that God is more important to us than anyone or anything else. In so doing, we invite the Holy Ghost to be a more personal motivator for us to constantly do good. As a result we can gain greater self-control over our weaknesses. Thus, isn't it worth it to live in total harmony with the Second Commandment? I think it is, and I hope you do also.

When was the last time that you personally tried to talk with God through personal prayer? When was the last time you really sought Him out to enter your life? If you have not done either of the above or have not done it for a long time, then have you let something else become more important to you than your Creator, your God, your very Father in Heaven? The molten gold calf at the time of Moses did not look like a god any more than money, pride, sex, tobacco, alcohol, drugs, and other various enticing "things" do today. However, there were many who did worship that molten gold calf. And, there are many more people today who worship their own various modern-day forms of the golden calf, or gods, instead of worshiping God the Father.

Have you in the past or are you presently offending God by breaking the Second Commandment? If you have, do something about it today! Keep reading, because this book can help guide you to becoming a much better person, regardless of how bad, or how good, you might presently appear to be.

If we appropriately worship God by keeping His commandments and doing good always, then look what He promises you and me: "...And showing mercy unto thousands of them that love, and keep my commandments." (Remember that when the Ten Commandments were given to Moses, there were not the billions of people on the earth that we have today). Now, if there is one thing that I would someday want from God, it is His mercy, especially at the Judgement Day. For if He gives me mercy, then He must love me. And, He will love me especially if I keep His commandments. The Second Commandment is as simple, as clear and as logical as that.

Thus, we must live and always keep His commandments, and demonstrate that we love Him through careful obedience to His commandments, if we are to be judged the way that we would like to be judged. Is there anyone out there who does not want to be judged with every ounce of mercy possible? The author does, because he knows he falls way short of being perfect, or of even being spotless. Jesus Christ, our Savior, was both perfect and spotless. But, we can become spotless some day through the spilled blood of Jesus Christ, if we do all we can to become worthy, which simply means that we must live according to all the commandments *(as best we can).*

If you have anything in your life that you are now worshipping more (paying more attention to) than God the Father and His son Jesus Christ, then I suggest that you immediately get on your knees and seek, maybe even beg, for forgiveness and strength through prayer. Do not go back even once to worshipping your old idols, images, statues, thoughts, actions or things.

3rd Commandment

"Thou shalt not take the name of the LORD thy God in vain; for the LORD will not hold him guiltless that taketh his name in vain." Exodus 20:7

Alicia wanted her boyfriend Jerry to do well in his first tennis match at the university. He was playing well, however in the third set he served a ball that hit the inside of the baseline, but was called out. Alicia looked at her girlfriend Janice and said, "Oh my G__, did you see that shot?" Meanwhile, Jerry became very angry at the line judge. He started yelling at him and said, "G__ damn it man, can't you see that ball was in?" In responding back to Larry, the line judge yelled, "No, Jesus C_____, couldn't you see it was out by an inch or two."

What do you think? Has Alicia broken the Third Commandment? Has Jerry broken the Third Commandment? Has the line judge broken the Third Commandment? Have they all broken the Third Commandment, or has just Jerry, or the line judge? Also, does one have to be angry in order to break this commandment? In short, "No," one does not have to be angry in order to break this commandment. But, Alicia, Jerry and the line judge have all broken the Third Commandment. Do you break the Third Commandment like Alicia, Jerry and the line judge did in the above case study?

The Third Commandment is probably broken more often than all the other commandments, with the possible exception of the breaking the Fourth Commandment of keeping the Sabbath day holy. This is due likely because most people unfortunately do not believe they really blaspheme or take the name of God in vain, although, in reality, they do. And it is done so often in today's society that most people don't even think about it, nor do they seem to care about it. Therein is a sad commentary, for the names of God and Jesus Christ are indeed sacred. I even have a problem in just writing down the misuse of Their names, as in the case study above.

To blaspheme or to speak the names of God and/or Jesus Christ in vain is to speak either name, or any of Their other names, outside of prayer, righteous songs or religious discussions. According to Webster's New World Dictionary, 1996 edition, to blaspheme is "to speak irreverently, or profanely of or about God or sacred things." It also means to "curse or revile." To profane means "not connected with religion or religious matters, not hallowed or consecrated, or showing disrespect or contempt for sacred things; irreverent." Generally speaking, blasphemy means irreverent or contemptuous speech concerning God or Jesus Christ. It also includes anything that is in a close sacred relationship to Them, such as a temple, church or synagogue, the commandments, the scriptures, or Their divine prophets and religious leaders.

People blaspheme the names of God and/or Jesus Christ, especially when they curse and swear. However, people also take Their holy names in vain when they are not angry, such as in the following statements, "Oh my G__!", or "Oh G__!", or "Oh L___!", or "Oh Jesus C_____!", offered as expressions of surprise or exclamation. These expressions, *as innocent as they may seem, certainly are irreverent and/or disrespectful. Thus, one does not have to be angry or cursing in order to blaspheme or to take the names of God and/or Jesus Christ in vain. One can just be irreverent or disrespectful in saying Their names and yet still be guilty of breaking the Third Commandment.* Again, the names of God and His son Jesus Christ are sacred, and we should always treat them as such (see Philippians 2:9-11). To do anything more than to say Their names only when it is appropriate, is to break the Third Commandment.

The breaking of this commandment is often done on national T.V., and yet today, most T.V. networks won't allow common swear words, let alone even mild cuss words to be said! But they do allow the sacred names of God the Father and Jesus Christ our Lord to be used in vain all the time! There are also many radio stations who are even worse than T.V. stations when it comes to allowing the names of God and Jesus Christ to be said in vain. And the individuals often think it is cute or hip to speak such things. What a mockery! What a joke! Satan has done a great job of seducing people of today into thinking that it is "no big thing" to utter the sacred names of God or Jesus Christ in vain. Satan has also done a good job in making people think they are not actually taking those sacred names in vain, when in reality, they are. It is a big thing. Why else would it be one of the Ten Commandments, if it weren't such "a big thing?

In the early days of Israel, to blaspheme or take the name of God in vain meant death by stoning. One such account is detailed in Leviticus, Chapter 24:10-23. The story involves an Israelitish woman whose son "blasphemed the name of the LORD and cursed." The people brought the blasphemer to Moses. (Whether he was an old son or a young son is not known, and may not be particularly important, but it would be interesting to know). Evidently, Moses then took the situation to the LORD. In His answer, the LORD commanded Moses to have the people "lay their hands upon his head, and let all the congregation stone him." In verse 15, Moses was further commanded:

"And thou shalt speak unto the children of Israel, saying, Whosoever curseth his God shall bear his sin."

To blaspheme in those days meant truly serious consequences. In Ezekiel 35:12-13, the LORD says that He hears "all thy blasphemies." And there is no doubt in the mind of the author that He hears those blasphemies as well today as He did at the time of Ezekiel. God even knows your thoughts (see Psalms 94:11 and 1st Corinthians 3:20), so if you even think Their names in vain without utterance, you are still guilty of breaking the Third Commandment.

It is interesting to note that after the scattering of the Twelve Tribes of Israel, the tribe of Judah continued their strict adherence to the Third Commandment. In fact, the Jews eventually would not even read the name of Jehovah in any of their private readings or their ceremonies and would substitute the name of Adoni instead. The name of Jehovah was indeed sacred then, as it is sacred today. The sad thing is that the Jehovah, the God of the Old Testament, is none other than Jesus Christ Himself, before He was born into mortality. What irony of ironies! (There is more about this subject later in the next chapter).

The subject of blasphemy was also considered serious in the New Testament. Two wonderful verses in Matthew 12:31-32 indicate that "All manner of sin and blasphemy shall be forgiven unto men:..." *but one must be careful to understand that in order to receive forgiveness, we must sincerely repent.* We have to change from sinning. Forgiveness is not something God gives freely without our sincere repentance and changing from within ourselves. To continue with the verses in Matthew, the Lord Jesus Christ states: "...but the blasphemy against the Holy Ghost shall not be forgiven unto men." In verse 32, *forgiveness from blasphemy or even speaking against the Holy Ghost, will not be extended to men, or women, in this world nor in the world to come.* Wow!

In Matthew 15:19, blasphemers are listed with such unsavory characters as murderers, adulterers, fornicators, stealers and lairs. To blaspheme the Lord's name is also referenced in Romans 2:24 and James 2:7. The seriousness of taking the names of God or Jesus Christ is great, even though you, your friends or others might never have considered it to be so.

Jesus Christ himself was often accused by the Jews of blasphemy when He indicated his rightful place and position as being the Son of God. The Lord Jesus Christ was also accused of blasphemy because He claimed the right to forgive sins (see Matthew 9:3, 26:65; Mark 2:5-12, and Luke 5:21-24), and because He said unto the Jews that they would see Him "sitting at the right hand of power, and coming in the clouds of heaven.", (see Matthew 26:64-65). In addition, the charge brought against Jesus by false witnesses before the Sanhedrin in Matthew 26:59-65 and John 19:8-12, was that of blasphemy against God's temple and that of actually being the Son of God. However, since Jesus Christ really was what and who He said He was, all the charges were false. I believe that those who brought the false charges have long regretted them, and will live a lot longer in the eternities with the same regret.

Jesus Christ had to suffer through all these terrible indignities from men who had little or no faith and certainly no spiritual knowledge. Yet, He was the author and the giver of the Ten Commandments to the children of Israel in the first place. An interesting irony, to be sure.

Today, since blasphemy is no big thing, and is so common today among people, especially the young, people do not hesitate to take in vain and blaspheme the names of God or Jesus Christ and to speak unholy about things that are sacred. The question should thus be asked: Are we being held today to the same standard in keeping the Third Commandment as were the people in the Old and New Testament times? In a word, yes! Well then, has the passage of time in any way diminished the power and the requirement for all of us to keep the commandments? No, it has not! And it will not change as time goes on. So, for all those who either willingly or knowingly break the commandments, there will be an accounting made of your disobedience. The accounting may not be in this world, but none-the-less, it will be made. You can count on it! Thus, woe be unto all who do not repent and begin to change their ways today from breaking any of the Twelve Commandments.

Everyone should remember that God is the title of our Heavenly Father. He is God, the Eternal Father, of all the universe. He is the God of all creation and his name is Elohim (see Chapter 1, verse 23 in the Talmad). And His son, the Lord Jesus Christ, is like unto God (see Hebrews 1:1-5 and 1st Corinthians 8:5-6). Jesus Christ is the God of the Old Testament and He was known as Jehovah, or the LORD (see Exodus 6:2-3, Isaiah 41:13-14, 43:11, 14-15 and John 8:56-58). He is also called by many other names as mentioned in both the Old and New Testaments. (Just a selected few of the many are, Seed of the woman, Genesis 3:15, with "it" in the Hebrew referring to "He," or actually Jesus Christ; I Am, Exodus 3:14-15; the Prophet, Deuteronomy 18:15-16 and John 7:40; Emmanuel, Isaiah 7:14, 8:8 and Matthew 1:23; Wonderful, Counselor, Mighty God, Everlasting Father, Prince of Peace, Isaiah 9:6; Lord, Savior, Redeemer, the mighty One of Jacob, Job 19:25, Isaiah 59:20, 60;16 and Jude 1:25; the Holy One of Israel, Isaiah 1:4 and 41:14; the Holy One and the Just, Acts 3:14; the image of God, 2nd Corinthians 4:4; Savior of Israel, Acts 13:23 and the Savior of the world, John 4:22). Jesus Christ is also correctly referred to as LORD or as God, our Lord and our God. He is the creator of this earth (see John 1:1-14 and Ephesians 3:9), and probably many other "earths" as well.

Jesus Christ's real father was not Joseph. Jesus was born of God, our Heavenly Father. Exactly how it happened, via the power and knowledge of God, is not important for us to know. What is important though, is to know and believe that it did happen. This is one of the main reasons why Jesus Christ was and still is so different from you and me, and was capable of doing the many wonderful things He did for us while on the earth. He was spotless and perfect in His earthly life (see Hebrews 5:8-9). And yet, Jesus Christ also had His free agency, as we do. He could have chosen in the preexistence to rebel as Satan did. He could have easily chosen to not condescend and come to this earth to be born and suffer in this life as He did, and to pay the awful price he paid through the Atonement and the Crucifixion. But thank goodness that He did, and that His life remains the one sterling and perfect example of ultimate faithfulness and obedience to God the Father, and to the promises He made in the pre-existence.

Jehovah gave the Ten Commandments to Moses, to all the Twelve Tribes of Israel, to you and me. When Jehovah was born unto the world to fulfill premortal promises, His name was, and still is, Jesus Christ (see Isaiah 41:13-14, 45:11-12, 49:26 and 54:5). Thus, "the Holy One of Israel," "the God of Jacob," "thy Saviour," "thy Redeemer," and "the God of the whole earth," are all the same, for they are none other than Jesus Christ! If you have carefully studied all the provided verses and prayed about it, you should now truly understand that Jehovah was none other than Jesus Christ. *His importance to this world from the beginning to the end, cannot be overstated.*

Jesus Christ later gave us the other Two Great Commandments. Actually, in importance, they are the First and Second Commandments, as found in Matthew 22:35-40, Mark 12:28-34 and Luke 10:25-37, which are addressed in greater detail later in the book.

Jesus Christ is also the creator of this earth (see Genesis 1:26; Psalms 33:6; Isaiah 40:28, 41:20, 42:5, 45:12; John 1:1-14, Acts 7:50; Ephesians 3:9; Col. 3:10; Heb. 1:2 and 1:10). He rightfully refers to himself in Isaiah 44:6 and 8, as the only God. This is true. He is in fact, the only God of this earth, thus, there is no other God of this earth other than Jehovah or Jesus Christ. He was the only creator of this earth, under direction and commandment of our Heavenly Father. However, just because we have Jehovah as the God of this earth, it in no way changes the fact that we, including Jesus Christ, are all spiritual children of our Heavenly Father, or God the Father. But again, remember, that Jesus Christ's earthly father was not

Joseph, but our Heavenly Father. Jesus Christ really was different from you and I, and thank goodness that He was. He was spotless and perfect in His earthly life, as no one has or ever will be. He set the perfect example for all of us to try and model. But as we can't really be perfect like Him in this life, we should none-the-less *try as best we can to be more like Him and to someday become spotless because of Him.* However, we can perfect our lives in many ways, especially with true repentance to help us.

The above paragraph begs the question, is Jehovah also the God of other planets like earth? (The author believes that He is, but that is an issue for another book). Suffice it to say that we are His. We are actually the property of Jesus Christ. He paid for us. He bought us and thus can redeem us from sin by His agonizing yet, most wonderful atoning sacrifice in Gethsemane. And with His final sacrifice on the cross, He gave us immortality through the power of the Resurrection. The Atonement coupled with the Resurrection give mankind the potential of having eternal life with God the Father and with Jesus Christ, *which is the ultimate blessing for all mankind.*

Throughout His life, Jesus Christ often referred with great reverence to His Father, the One that sent Him (see Luke 2:49 and John 6:25-40). This is God, the Eternal Father, the Father of every earthly spirit. In Matthew 5:16, Jesus commanded us to "Let your light so shine before men, that they may see your good works, and glorify your Father which is in Heaven." Also, in Matthew 5:48, "Be ye therefore perfect, even as your Father which is in heaven is perfect.", we are reminded again and again that Jesus Christ was further reminding us that we all have the same Father. Although God the Father is Jesus Christ's spiritual as well as His literal Father, God is also our spiritual Father. God the Father is the Father of all spirits. Jesus says many times to us in the New Testament, "...your Father." He is referring to that Father who sent Him to the earth, is also the same Father who sent us to earth. In Acts 17:28-29, it reads:

> ***"For in him we live, and move and have our being; as certain also of your own poets have said, For we are also his offspring. Forasmuch then as we are the offspring of God, we ought not to think that the Godhead is like unto gold, or silver, or stone, graven by art and man's device."***

We are told plainly by the Apostle Paul in the statement above that we all are literally the offspring of God. We are all, in fact, made in His image.

The mission of Jesus Christ on earth was to fulfill the work that the Father had given Him to complete (see John 5:36-37, 43, 6:37-40, 44). And Jesus Christ's work consisted of literally setting and teaching the proper examples of life for us, providing us the plan of salvation for potential eternal life with Him and Heavenly Father, atoning for all of our repented sins, thus paving the way for that eternal life, and then resurrecting Himself to give us immortality. All these things He did in His always perfect example, in His wonderful teachings, and especially in the Atonement at Gethsemane, in His death on Golgotha and in His Resurrection two days later from the tomb. It is Jesus Christ alone who can save us from the death of the grave. It is Jesus Christ alone who can pave the way for us to someday return to our Father in Heaven in a spotless condition to potentially inherit eternal life with both of Them.

Jesus Christ provided the Resurrection for everyone, to both the good and the bad. (Read again John 6:39). None shall be lost. Everyone will be resurrected! It is free to everyone who has ever lived or even yet to live on the earth. This is the "grace" of Jesus Christ. We will all be resurrected, even if we don't want to be! It seems to me that to be resurrected and yet have lived a wicked life on earth would be a terribly difficult conflict for one to experience during the eternities. This is because a resurrected body is a pure body, one designed to live forever, but not necessarily guaranteed to have eternal life with our Father in Heaven and Jesus Christ.

Living forever or everlasting life is *different* from having eternal life with Heavenly Father and Jesus Christ. Various christian sects teach they are the same, but they are not! Someone living in a pure resurrected body with a history of unrepented wickedness will live forever, but not in the presence of God the Father and Jesus Christ. It will be impossible. That great blessing has been reserved for those repentant souls who have accomplished many works of righteousness and become worthy, of which a strong belief in Jesus Christ being the son of God, and then baptism by one having the proper authority, being the first two steps (John 3:1-7). This discussion illustrates why there will be a second and a third resurrection, to come after the morning of the first resurrection, wherein the righteous are to be resurrected. The second resurrection for the less righteous will take place in the afternoon after the first resurrection. The third resurrection and any additional ones for the wicked, will take place only after the millennial reign (one thousand years) of Jesus Christ is over. The wicked will thus be denied a resurrection for a thousand years!

Maybe this thousand year time period is designed so the wicked can work on their spiritual and behavioral inadequacies as well as pay the terrible price for their unrepentant sins. And all this is in preparation to eventually receive their personal scary presentation and judgement before the Father by Jesus Christ.

The first resurrection is reserved for the righteous of the earth. We thus will not all be resurrected at the same time and to the same resurrection (see 1st Corinthians 15:12-29, 39-43 and Revelation 20:1-15). Any and all other resurrections than the first are reserved for those not so righteous. As for the author and his family and friends, and he is sure there are many others, we are all trying hard to be members of the first resurrection. How about YOU? Which resurrection do you want to have? Think about it very carefully. Are your personal works of righteousness or wickedness important? Yes, you can bet your future and eternal happiness on it.

It is during life on earth that we are to prepare for the morning of the first resurrection. Of course, there is still time to repent and change, at least there is before you die. To avoid the conflict of having a resurrected body but having lived a wicked life as mentioned above, it thus becomes so important to live a good and righteous life while yet still on the earth. Righteous living is important that your condition both during the Resurrection and life thereafter will be a happy and glorious one. However, if you have not lived such a life up until right now, then it is even more important that you begin to repent and change, this very day. Start now to sincerely determine to change from your past sinful behavior and begin living a righteous life from this day on without returning to any of those former negative, inappropriate or sinful behaviors.

The saving grace of Jesus Christ goes much further than just the Resurrection. Jesus Christ provided the Atonement for everyone, as He did the Resurrection. However, the wonderful resulting blessings from the Atonement, of eternal life with Heavenly Father and Jesus Christ, is *conditional.* This is unlike the total application condition of the Resurrection.

The horrible suffering that Jesus Christ experienced while in Gethsemane, where I believe He actually did sweat great drops of blood for you and me, was even greater than what He suffered on the cross. In fact, the intensity of His suffering in Gethsemane evidently surprised even Christ Himself, as indicated in Mark 14:33-34 and Luke 22:43-44.

Even though Jesus Christ's terrible suffering and eventual death on the cross was actually secondary to that of Gethsemane, they were none-the-less critical and necessary for the resurrection of all mankind. Although Jesus Christ was unique in that no one could ever take His life, *He had to give it up voluntarily.* According to the scripture in Psalms 69:20-21, it was prophesied long before it happened that Jesus Christ would actually die of a broken heart:

"Reproach hath broken my heart; and I am full of heaviness: and I looked for some to take pity, but there was none; and for comforters, but I found none. They gave me also gall for my meat; and in my thirst they gave me vinegar to drink."

In addition, research conducted by Dr. William Stroud in his work *On the Physical Cause of the Death of Christ,* and the Apostle John's writing of "...came there out blood and water.", (John 19:34), confirm that Jesus Christ actually did die of a broken heart.

(In fairly rare occurrences where the heart ruptures, blood evidently accumulates in the pericardium, or the lining around the heart, and then the corpuscles separate into a separate mass leaving a watery somewhat colorless serum. Thus, we have the "... blood and water." statement that John reported).

Keep in mind that it was *only* the sinless Jesus Christ who could suffer the pains that He suffered in Gethsemane and yet live, live for the crucifixion later on that frightful day! No one that has ever lived on the earth or will yet live on the earth could have lived through what Jesus Christ suffered, especially in Gethsemane. His suffering was so great, as he bled from every pore, because He took upon Himself all the sins of the world, even those sins yet to be committed. *And He suffered both in Gethsemane and on Golgotha during the same day, and it was wonderfully done for you and me!*

A most interesting thought about all the above is that Jesus Christ had His free agency, just like you and I have, and could have elected not to suffer and die for us. But nevertheless, He did suffer so greatly and then triumphantly complete His work with His voluntary death on the cross, *and we can all be forever so very thankful that He did. We thus are His.*

He did for us what we could not do for ourselves. Every person born on this earth will be eternally in debt to Jesus Christ for His Atonement and Resurrection. And the best way, to *at least* try to repay Him, is to be obedient to His commandments and to conform our behavior more to what His behavior would be. Think of what the world would be like if everyone did this.

Can you imagine the greatness of His love for us and His commitment to us? Actually, His love and commitment to us go beyond the capability of our finite minds to truly understand and appreciate. How is it possible then, to ever speak His name, or the name of His Father, and our Heavenly Father, in vain ever again? Or, how is it possible to blaspheme *anything* that They stand for? Keep the above in mind the next time you are tempted to speak Their holy names in vain or to blaspheme Their names. Remembering the above should be helpful to all mankind.

It is very interesting to revisit and try to understand the greatness of the pain and suffering Jesus Christ suffered in Gethsemane, which surprised even Himself. As stated in Mark 14:33-34, the Savior "...began to be sore amazed, and to be very heavy." Further, "And saith unto them, My soul is exceeding sorrowful unto death:..." In Luke 22:44, it states that Jesus Christ "And being in an agony he prayed more earnestly:..." How was it possible that the Savior of the world needed to pray more earnestly, unless it was critical for Him to do so? And of course, it was.

The author feels that of prime concern on the Savior's part was that He felt He might not be able to fulfill this terrible and awesome task that He was destined to do, but not forced to fulfill. In addition, Satan was likely throwing every temptation he had to throw at the Savior at this extremely critical period of time. All this likely resulted in the Savior's pleading in the three separate requests to the Father "that the cup might pass from me." (see Matthew 26:36-46, Mark 14:32-42 and Luke 22:39-46). But that wonderful word, "nevertheless," and thank goodness for it, the Father saw fit that Jesus Christ would be triumphant *on his own* in this terribly important time for you and me. The Father actually withdrew His presence and strength from Jesus Christ while He hung on the cross. The Savior, thus felt the absence of the Father when He uttered the words: "Eli, Eli, lama sabachthani?", which means, "My God, my God, why has thou forsaken me?". The Father wanted to insure that His precious Son, the Savior Jesus Christ, would alone, *on his own*, triumph over sin and death. Thus, *no one* will ever be able to say or even imply that Christ was only able to do what He did because of His Father's help. It was Christ's victory alone, and it will be remembered as such through out the eternities.

And thank goodness that Jesus Christ exceedingly well measured up to the most awesome of all tasks; that He alone was totally triumphant. For His complete personal victories over humanity's sins and the death of the body, resulted in His ability to eventually make us spotless. But this is only after we repent, *not just believe*, and afterwards live the commandments. Then, and only then, Christ hopefully will forgive us and present us to the Father for judgement for possible eternal life with Himself and Heavenly Father (see Matthew 1:21, 20:28, 26:28, John 5:18-22, 14:6-7, 11-12, 21, and 1st John 2:1).

The author is aware of a few statements in the New Testament where we are told that one only has to believe in God and Jesus Christ in order to be "saved" (see John 3:36; 5:24; 11:25 and Romans 1:16). However, by the grace of Jesus Christ we are *already* "saved" from eternal death via the Resurrection, whether we believe it or not! However, there will be many who will greatly limit their growth in righteousness and worthiness by *just* believing. But those who truly understand and who really want to live in the presence of the Father and the Son on an eternal basis, know they must not only believe, they know they must also work hard to become more righteous and worthy so that they might become spotless by way of Jesus Christ. (The reader is referred to James, Chapter 2, for a great discussion as to how important good works are in the process of becoming worthy. One cannot demonstrate real faith without doing good works!) Consider the purpose of the Judgement. It is then when our works on this earth will be determinded to be righteous or otherwise, and we will be judged and rewarded appropriately.

Contemplate for a minute what the consequences might be for you and me, and everyone else who has ever lived or will yet live on earth, if Jesus Christ had failed or that He did not love us enough to complete those last three critical events, the Atonement, the Crucifixion and the Resurrection. Wow! The thought makes reason stare! The author hopes that you now have a greater appreciation for the greatness and wonderfulness of the Savior Jesus Christ, for He did all that He did because He loves you and me. He really does love *you*. There is no other reason to fully explain all that He has done and will yet do for you and me, and everyone else.

In any case, it was a supreme and eternal sacrifice that He made for each of us in Gethsemane. He literally paid for us through His blood shedding and suffering for all our sins. He bought us! He paid for us! We are His, like it or not. But now we can *rejoice greatly*, for His sacrifice is sufficient. It can eventually allow us all to someday live with Jesus Christ and Heavenly Father, and experience what is in store for all those who have become worthy enough to obtain that most wonderful of all blessings. Again, that blessing is of eternal life with Jesus Christ and Heavenly Father (see 1st Corinthians 2:9).

It was earlier stated that the blessings of eternal life and living with Heavenly Father and Jesus Christ are conditional. *They are conditional upon personal worthiness.* They are NOT free gifts; and again, it takes a lot more than just believing, as much as Satan and others would like you to believe, that "belief" alone is all it takes to be "saved" or to gain eternal life. If you really believe in Jesus Christ as your Savior, then you *must* do as He commands, and He has commanded us many times in the New Testament to repent and become worthy of Him so that He can become our personal Savior. *One becomes worthy by repenting and being immersed and baptized by one having authority, and by changing from the natural man to a more spiritual man or woman; by progressing from grace to grace; by working hard and progressing little-by-little in becoming a better person each day of your life. We must also be active in helping others. In essence, we must live according to all Twelve of the Commandments as best we can while we are still living on this earth.*

For us to inherit from the Atonement what the Father has reserved for us, is to inherit *everything* He has to offer (see Revelations 21:7-8). The Atonement is about much more than just "being saved." It also requires much more from each one of us than "just believing" in Jesus Christ. *If one carefully studies the scriptures, one will come to clearly understand that to believe on His name is to do all that He has commanded us to do, not to just believe!* This is a serious point which the reader must thoroughly understand. Jesus Christ wants us to be doers of the word, not just hearers or just believers! There are significant differences between "doers" and "believers." We thus, must work hard and overcome our weaknesses and shortcomings in order to be worthy to inherit the blessings of the Atonement. We can do this by our doing all that we can *to become worthy in this life, by living the commandments, by becoming a much better person and by always helping others.* Then, because of the Atonement, Jesus Christ can make us spotless, not perfect, but spotless from sin in order to be presented to our Father in Heaven at the time of judgement (see Revelation 20:12-15). (We will work on perfection throughout the eternities). We have to become spotless first via true repentance and the grace of Jesus Christ before we can be presented to the Father by Jesus Christ and someday in the future life, become perfect. We have to first be spotless (cleansed from sin) because we are commanded to be perfect in Matthew 5:48, "Be ye perfect, even as your Father which is in heaven is perfect." And in Ephesians 5:5, "For this ye know, that no whoremonger, nor unclean person, nor covetous man, who is an idolater, hath any inheritance in the kingdom of Christ and of God," we learn that no unclean thing can have an inheritance in the kingdom of God the Father and His son Jesus Christ, whether we are a "believer" or not! Again, *we must be doers of the word, not just hearers or just believers.*

It is only through Jesus Christ that we can become clean and presentable to our Father in Heaven. But we must always be actively involved in doing good things for others and in perfecting our own personal behavior. When we repent, we change little by little those behaviors which are not proper in the sight of God or Jesus Christ. And as long as we do not return to those inappropriate behaviors, as gross as they may have been, with the possible exception of willful murder and for sure, blaspheme against the Holy Ghost, then we will be making righteous progress. And righteous progress is what our life should be about. That should be our dedication in life, to our Creator and to His son, our Savior, Jesus Christ.

When we become spotless, we are enabled to partake in the most wonderful blessing of eternal life with Heavenly Father and Jesus Christ. In this life we will make mistakes in our quest to be worthy, and Satan will do all he can to destroy each of us in the process. However, as you and I make repentance a normal part of our behavior, we will then make righteous progress, thus making fewer mistakes as time goes forward. I believe this is what our Heavenly Father and Jesus Christ want us to do; to *make righteous progress*. And we do this by becoming a better person who is more humble, forgiving, caring, thoughtful, unselfish, obedient to the commandments, kinder and gentler and generally a much more righteous person.

In my mind, to inherit anything less than eternal life with Heavenly Father and Jesus Christ would be "Hell," and I think that is what Hell really is. It is to eternally be without God our Father and His beloved son Jesus Christ, or to be denied entry into the place where They are. I hope you agree and are willing to make any necessary changes in your life in order to start on your quest to obtain eternal life with Heavenly Father and Jesus Christ. Start today! And you don't need to send money to me, or a preacher, minister or evangelist in order to do it. Through your own dedicated study and prayers, and with the help of the Holy Ghost, you can make dramatic changes within yourself. If you really believe you can receive the help, and if you consciously fast and pray about it in the name of Jesus Christ, the help will come.

If you do all the right things, the expected good results will happen. Maybe not in your time frame, but through faith, they will happen.

Now, in order for us to merit the full effects of His Atonement, not the Resurrection which again, is free to all of us, we must not only repent and change our behavior, but we must also be baptized. This baptism must be a full immersion baptism, as was Jesus Christ's baptism. We must also be baptized into the Kingdom of God by one having the proper priesthood authority, as the scriptures testify in Mark 1:1-11, Luke 2:1-8, Mark 16:16, John 3:3-7, Acts 2:37-38, Matthew 28:18-20 and Colossians 2:12. We then will be ready to have the gift of the Holy Ghost conferred upon us, again, by one who has the proper priesthood authority to do such. *We must then live as indicated above, all the commandments as best we can for the rest of our lives.* This means we must endure all that is thrown at us by Satan, or even given to us as challenges from God, until our time on earth is finished. That is quite a challenge isn't it? But it can be done. There are many in this world today who are presently doing it. *So can you!*

Remember, especially if you are unfamiliar with the process of repentance and real behavioral change, that it takes time and must be carefully done over a period of time. The basic principles of repentance are:

1) godly sorrow for what you have done.
2) confession to God in prayer, and if serious enough, to your religious leader and to those you have wronged,
3) making restitution as best you can, and then,
4) never, repeating the sin(s) again.

In John 1:9, it states,

> ***"If we confess our sins, he is faithful and just to forgive us our sins and to cleanse us from all unrighteousness."***

The beauty of the Savior's forgiveness is wonderful. However, you should remember to complete all the above steps diligently, because through them we really can demonstrate our willingness to change our sinful behavior. Also, seek guidance not only from your religious leaders on this issue, but especially seek help through dedicated fasting and prayer to the Father, said in the name of Jesus Christ (see Matthew 7:7-8, Luke 11:9-10 and John 15:16). *You will receive spiritual promptings from the Holy Ghost and be provided the direction in which you should go and the things you should do.* If you need specific counseling, seek out only those counselors who have the priesthood, are righteous, spiritual and sensitive to things of the spirit and testify of the divinity of Jesus Christ. *Also, don't be afraid or too scared to talk to dedicated missionaries who have the priesthood and who officially represent and bear testimony of Jesus Christ.* They just may have the "good news message" that you need.

Now, when you or any of your friends or family members utter the names of God or Jesus Christ in anything *other* than in prayer, in righteous song or in religious discussions, you and they really are saying those holy names in vain. It is hoped that you now have a much greater understanding and appreciation for the sacredness of the names of God the Father and Jesus Christ. Now, go about teaching your friends about these truths.

Breaking any of the Twelve Commandments is a serious sin. If you or your friends or family members personally need to take this Third Commandment much more seriously, then please do so immediately, and then change the future way you speak about your Savior and His Father, your Spiritual Father as well. Remember that when you speak Their names in the future, say Them appropriately with great reverence, love, respect and appreciation.

If you have trouble keeping this commandment and are saying Their sacred names in vain without realizing it, make yourself aware and then count each time you say Their name(s). Reduce the number of times down each week until you say Them no more, *except in prayer, in righteous song or in religious discussion.* As a helpful and sharp reminder, put a loose rubber band on your wrist and snap it each time immediately when you utter one of the sacred names. Do not hesitate to ask for assistance and reminders from your friends in your daily battle to keep the Third Commandment.

4th Commandment

"Remember the sabbath day, to keep it holy. Six days shalt thou labour, and do all thy work: But the seventh day is the sabbath of the LORD thy God: in it thou shalt not do any work, thou, nor thy son, nor thy daughter, thy maidservant, nor thy cattle, nor thy stranger that is within thy gates: For in six days the LORD made heaven and earth, the sea and all that in them is and rested the seventh day: wherefore the LORD blessed the sabbath day, and hallowed it." Exodus 20:8-11

Toby and his family had been invited by Toby's boss, Bill Webster and his family, to go boating on the Columbia River and then go to the county fair to experience all the crazy and wild rides. When Toby told his family of the invitation, Toby's mother reminded him that the Webster's wanted to go on Sunday. Toby said, "So what, Mom?" Toby's mother then took the time to remind Toby that it was not appropriate to do any of those things on the Sabbath day. Toby argued with his mother and said he was going to go with the Websters anyway.

Do you think that going boating and then to the county fair on Sunday is okay? Or would it be breaking the Fourth Commandment? Yes, if Toby goes with the Websters, he, along with all the Websters, will break the Fourth Commandment.

In the above example, what if Toby's boss had required him to work on Sunday? If Toby was to work on Sunday, would he again be breaking the Fourth Commandment? Technically speaking, Toby would be breaking the commandment; however, he would likely not be held accountable since he had no control over what his boss required. However, if it bothered Toby enough, and it should, he should get another job that did not require him to work on the Sabbath.

In the Old Testament, working on the Sabbath day was cause for death. The Lord meant business when He gave Israel the Fourth Commandment to keep the Sabbath day holy. There are evidently additional reasons why keeping the day holy is mandatory other than it just being the seventh day of the week when Monday is counted as the first day of the week. In Exodus, Chapter 31:15-17, it says:

> ***"Six days may work be done; but in the seventh is the sabbath of rest, holy to the LORD: whosoever doeth any work in the sabbath day he shall surely be put to death. Wherefore the children of Israel shall keep the sabbath, to observe the sabbath throughout their generations, for a perpetual covenant. It is a sign between me and the children of Israel for ever: for in six days the LORD made heaven and earth, and on the seventh day he rested, and was refreshed."***

We are part of those "generations," and are thus obligated to keep that "perpetual covenant." And the Sabbath day is a sign of that "perpetual covenant," which lasts forever! Wow! Forever is definitely a long, long, time.

The Fourth Commandment is interesting in two special ways. The first is that in Matthew 12:1-9, Mark 2:23-28, Mark 3:1-5 and Luke 6:1-12, it is apparent that Jesus Christ is the Lord who originally gave the Sabbath-day commandment as Jehovah. He is the Lord of the Sabbath day, man is not. Although, it is also apparent that the Sabbath day was instituted to commemorate a day of rest for Jehovah after His creations were completed during the six previous days. It was also a day created for man. (Remember that a day for God is equivalent to a thousand years for man. See 2nd Peter 3:8). However, this verse seems to be taken literaly by some and figuratvely by others. The Sabbath day was a day made for all people to take a break from everyday activities, to focus on more spiritual things, to worship God and to do good things for others. The Sabbath day is a special, sacred and holy day and should be treated as such by everyone. It is not necessarily a day of sleep!

Jesus Christ was often falsely accused by the Jews of breaking the Sabbath day. However, Jesus was always consistent in not only doing what the Father wanted Him to do, but also in keeping the Sabbath day holy, as we shall determine later in the text. And so should we keep it holy, even in this day and period of time. *We have not outgrown the requirement to live the Fourth Commandment!*

In three Gospels of the New Testament, Jesus Christ asked those around him, including the Pharisees, if it was lawful to heal or to do good on the Sabbath day (see Matthew 12:8, 12, Mark 2:27-28, 3:3-5 and Luke 6:6-10). There evidently were no answers in response to the question asked in any of the accounts, thus, Jesus Christ quite appropriately proclaimed himself to be the Lord of the Sabbath day and He then healed a man in the synagogue who had a withered hand. But Jesus, as outlined especially in the Luke reference, was totally consistent within the spirit, intent and letter of the Sabbath day commandment. The main reason that the Jews became so infuriated as they accused Him of breaking the

Sabbath day commandment, was that He refused to conform to the traditions and the added regulations the Jewish elders themselves had made over the years concerning Sabbath day observance (see Matthew 15:1-9 and Mark 7:1-13).

It really is interesting to note that Jesus Christ as the Jehovah of the Old Testament, was the one who actually gave the commandements to Moses. He certainly showed them well, as opposed to the Jewish leaders.

There are additional accounts in the four Gospels where Jesus is accused of breaking the Sabbath, and, of course, He never did. In addition, as Jesus Christ has well demonstrated, it is okay to do good on the Sabbath, but it still is not appropriate to work on the Sabbath day!

Jesus did, in fact, obey both the letter and spirit of the law of the Sabbath day. There is no doubt in the mind of the author that the Sabbath day is an eternal principle and has always existed with God the Father, and likely existed with man from the time of Adam, and whenever the gospel was with man on the earth. Thus, the Great Jehovah of the Old Testament as Jesus Christ of the New Testament, could do nothing else but observe the Sabbath day as an eternal principle, and thus Himself faithfully keep his own Fourth Commandment.

It is interesting to note that sometime after the resurrection of Jesus Christ, members of the Church, probably both Jews and Gentiles, started keeping holy the first day of the week. This was likely done as a weekly memorial or commemoration of our Lord's resurrection. Little by little the observance of the seventh day by calendar count was discontinued. However, it needs to be stressed that the change from observing the last day of the week to the first day of the week (Sunday), is not so important as is the principle and spirit of the Sabbath. Besides, which Roman or Greek leader "officially" decided that the day of Sunday was actually the first day of the week rather than the seventh? Most importantly, it should be remembered that the Sabbath was symbolic of a day of rest following the wonderful six days of work in the creation of this earth, the deliverance of Israel from Egypt, and the resurrection of Jesus Christ from the grave. Man, thus works six days and then rests on the seventh day. It becomes more a matter of count, as to which day one wishes to call the first day of the week or the last day of the week.

As the author, I am comfortable in observing Sunday as the appropriate Sabbath day. Sunday comes at the end of a week of work. Sunday also seems to fit the creation plan the best and certainly is a glorious day in which to appropriately celebrate the resurrection of the Lord. But, what really matters is that we have one day in seven in which the Sabbath is officially observed. We thus, preserve especially the spirit of the law. On the other hand, today, most people don't observe a Sabbath day anyway, regardless of what day of the week it is! So the argument of whether Sunday is actually the first or the seventh day of the week becomes somewhat of a moot point.

There are other references the reader is encouraged to look up and read concerning the Sabbath day in the New Testament. They are Luke 13:11-17, 14:1-6, John 5:18, 7:14-24, Romans 14:5-6 and Colossians 2:16. In the ninth chapter of John, Jesus is again accused of violating the Sabbath day by healing a blind man. He then lectures the Jews for their spiritual blindness. However, even with all the references as cited above, one who studies the scriptures might think that such an important subject as the Sabbath day should have far more references in the New Testament, especially for those who willingly break it.

It is my opinion that the reason why there seems to be such a lack of more specific verses concerning faithful observance of the Sabbath day in the New Testament, is due to the day being so universally honored and respected in ancient times. There really was little need for reminders. Most everyone in the 12 tribes of Israel lived in accordance with appropriate behavior on the Sabbath day. This situation is probably similar for the first three commandments, since they also are not mentioned much in the New Testament. It was probably very hard to contemplate not observing the Sabbath, even from those Gentiles who did not have the strict laws the Jews had. On the other hand, who could have foreseen our day when we have open rebellion in keeping the Sabbath day holy? I am quite sure that God could have foreseen it, but generally, the writers of the books in the New Testament evidently did not, or at least they did not write about it to any great extent.

You should also understand the likely reasons why Jesus Christ did not mention the Sabbath day commandment when asked by a young man as to which commandments to live after being told by Jesus Christ to "keep the commandments" (see Matthew 19:16-26; Mark 10:17-22; Luke 18:18-30). The first likely reason, as mentioned above, being that the Sabbath was so universally practiced that there was no need to mention it. Again, this is the same likely reason why the first three of the original Ten Commandments were also not mentioned. (To not covet was also not mentioned). The second likely reason, which is closely tied to the first, is that the five commandments mentioned, plus "to love thy neighbor as thy self," mentioned only in the Matthew account, were probably the commandments most likely not being well followed at that time. However, the reader should not think for even a moment that the unmentioned five commandments were somehow made less important or done away. They were still in force then and they are all still in force today! We will all be judged according to all the original Ten Commandments in the Old Testament.

The importance of the Sabbath day as a day of rest from everyday labors, to contemplate the word of the Lord and assemble together for worship are major factors in the spiritual development of mankind. In addition, *history will testify that the moral decay of a society most often follows decreased observance of the sacredness of the Sabbath day.* The consistent observance of a weekly holy day is one of society's most important safeguards. It serves as a weekly reminder that we are all God's children and that we are in constant need of His help, blessings and revelations. It also serves as a quiet witness that there is indeed such a thing as "on-going revelation."

It is no wonder that Satan has done such a great "slam dunk" on people today in convincing them that the Sabbath is a day of play and entertainment and not a day of worship and rest from worldly things. Wow! We are ripe for destruction. It is my opinion that the general lack of honoring the Sabbath day is one of mankind's greatest mistakes. Coupled with the overall gross absence of reverence and honor for God the Father and Jesus Christ, the general lack of honoring the Sabbath day constitute two of the gravest collective sins that mankind can make, and mankind is presently doing a "great job" with both of them.

In New Testament times, Jesus reasoned well with those who tried to accuse Him that it was breaking the Fourth Commandment to heal and do good on the Sabbath day. His logic as found in the references of Matthew, Mark, Luke, and John cannot be argued with, in that it is within the spirit of the Sabbath to do good, and that is what He did in healing the man with the withered hand and healing others as well.

We are reminded again that one can be sure that God the Father and Jesus Christ will always be consistent in keeping all the commandments They give to us on earth. Also, there will never be inconsistencies in Their behavior. They behave the same today and forever. *It is only in man where inconsistent behavior is possible.* God and Jesus Christ will never break covenants but man surely does.

The second way in which the Fourth Commandment is interesting is that it is an easy commandment to break and quite a difficult one to keep, especially today. There is also a lot of gray area with this commandment. As mentioned earlier, Satan loves to have you struggle in the "gray area," where the appropriate and righteous way is not clearly evident, and it is a struggle to find it. But, find it we must and we do it by inviting divine help.

In the early days of the Old Testament, the Jews evidenced that they could not handle those higher laws which included some "gray areas." This is essentially why God gave the Jews, through Moses, such strict lower-level rules of performance and ceremony to obey. And devout Jews of today are still trying to keep those strict rules, made even more strict by various Jewish leaders over the years. This is still done so even though these old rules of performance and ceremony in the Mosaic Law were long ago fulfilled and done away with by the life and death of Jesus Christ. However, the original Ten Commandments, which were part of the basic law including faith, repentance, baptism in water for the remission of sins, *were not rescinded or done away with.* This is true because Jesus Christ taught them all in the New Testament. The Jews of today, as well as the rest of humanity, are all still required to keep the Fourth Commandment, as well as the rest of the Twelve Commandments.

There are many today who are confused as to why they should keep the Sabbath day holy. I recently talked to a young Christian man who owns a bicycle shop in Portland, Oregon, but keeps it open on Sunday. I asked him how it was possible for him to be a "born-again" practicing Christian and yet be open on Sunday. He surprisingly said he was not in violation of the Sabbath day commandment. He mistakenly believed that since Jesus did away with much of the Law of Moses, He evidently did away with the Ten Commandments. The young man could not specify as to which ones were deleted other than the Fourth Commandment. I have tried to get him to turn his thinking around, for he mistakenly thinks the Ten Commandments were the Law of Moses. *The Ten Commandments were only part of the Law of Moses and they were not done away with, as were the various laws of carnal commandments and ceremony, as well as blood sacrifices.* Yet this young man is symptomatic of what many people generally, but incorrectly, believe in this country, as well as in other parts of the world. People do not understand. Additionally, they will not even listen to real understanding when it is clearly presented to them.

Jesus Christ did not do away with the Ten Commandments. They still apply to us today! People will sometimes read a few scriptures, or have someone tell them something about the scriptures and they will then falsely believe without any study, fasting or prayer. Again, this young man seems to be missing an important point, just like the Jews did of old, and yet he professes to be a "born again Christian!" (I am still working with this young man to help him read, study, pray and fast more carefully. In so doing, he will hopefully receive the greater light and want to change his thinking, and thus keep the Sabbath day holy by closing his shop on Sunday).

Generally, what does it actually mean to keep the Sabbath day holy? *It essentially means that we should be doing much less of the things of worldly man and concentrate much more on the things of God.* We should not go shopping or patronize retail or wholesale businesses on Sunday. There is more than enough time during the week to shop and buy things. It also means that we do not go to sporting events or other entertainment such as movies, or other recreational events on Sunday. Wow! Think what that would do to the world of professional sports and to the world of rock concerts? It also means that if we own a business we should not require any of our employees to work on Sunday. Shudder! And yet many stores make much of their money from shoppers on Sunday.

Keeping the Sabbath day holy also means that we do not go fishing, hunting, trapping, hiking, horseback riding, boating, skiing, biking, golfing, play baseball, play basketball, play football, play soccer, go to the movie or rodeo, shop, do yard work, go to games, go to the circus or ice skating rink and many other recreational things we presently do on Sunday. If you do not do the above things on Sunday, the more power to you and give yourself a big pat on the back for keeping the Fourth Commandment. You evidently have invited the Holy Ghost into your life, and by doing so you know by the Spirit what to do to keep the Sabbath day holy, and more importantly, you actually do those appropriate things. But, if you do those things mentioned above and/or things like them on Sunday, then you are invited by the author to seriously think and plan to change what you do on the next Sunday, and every Sunday thereafter. You are invited to do those things which are consistent with the Sabbath day. *You are invited to become a more godly person and appropriately observe the Sabbath day.*

Now that you know of things not to do on the Sabbath, just what things can you do on Sunday and yet keep it holy? First, we can all go to church. Everyone needs to go to a house of worship on Sunday. A house of worship is where the Spirit should be felt, and if you don't feel the Spirit, then go to one wherein you do. We are to be edified and lifted up, actually made better because of our attending houses of worship. Also, dedicated prayer is a great practice for the Sabbath. The Sabbath day is the day set aside by the Lord for doing the things of the Lord, *not* the things of man. You can do good, as the Savior taught, by visiting the sick, and talking and reading to the old and the lonely. How long has it been since you have done one of the above worthy things? Sunday is a wonderful day to do them. You are encouraged to do much good on the Sabbath day, especially if it involves serving others.

You can also read good uplifting books and articles on the Sabbath day, especially the scriptures. There needs to be more dedicated reading and study from the Bible, the Koran, the Torah, and other great religious books you may not be familiar with. People today do not have a love of reading like people did of yesterday. Why is there not as much reading being done today? The author feels that it is principally because of T.V. In fact, as a society we have given in to T.V. There is more time wasted while watching T.V. than with any other activity within the last 50 years. Many of our youth as well as many adults have been destroyed by this monster. And yet it is so easy to control. *Just don't turn it on!* Or since this might be a difficult thing to do because there are some good things on T.V., just carefully monitor what you and your family watch. Shows like "Touched by an Angel," nature shows, Public Broadcasting Station presentations and some balanced news broadcasts are usually excellent and should be watched. But, don't waste your time watching the soaps or watching those horrible talk shows, which often titillate and try to shock their viewers with their bizarre programming. (In the author's opinion, the only exceptions possibly being The Oprah Winfrey and the Dr. Phil Shows. Their shows are several notches above all the other talk shows on T.V. They concentrate on social issues that usually uplift and edify mankind, not on issues that denigrate and glorify the inappropriate behaviors of mankind). Substitute reading uplifting and motivational magazines and books for the soaps and the talk shows other than Oprah's and Dr. Phil's.

With the advent of the VCR, digital recorders, DVDs and computers, people can now watch a variety of movies and recorded events in their home. Is it appropriate to watch movies on Sunday? We should certainly not go out to attend movies at the movie house on Sunday, but can we still watch a movie? This is again one of those "gray areas" referred to in an earlier section.

If the movie or event is uplifting and leads to good positive and uplifting feelings, then you are probably within the spirit of the Sabbath day. However, if the movie is rated “PG-13” or worse, or is violent, sexy, nasty, or disturbing, then it is not in keeping with the Sabbath day. Of course, those kinds of movies are inappropriate on any day of the week and should not be viewed for any reason. Because of watching them, you will drive the uplifting spirit of the Holy Ghost away from you, and once gone it is sometimes hard to get back.

As you grow in your knowledge and appreciation of the Sabbath day, you will have greater strength to make better decisions as to what you should do and not do on the Sabbath day. Make a strong effort to analyze your Sabbath-day activities and then make them consistent within the spirit of the Sabbath day.

On the Sabbath day you can also communicate with far-away family or friends through letters, phone calls, or even through E-mail. You can listen to uplifting music in your home. When was the last time you listened to the Mormon Tabernacle Choir, The Messiah, or a symphony or a piano or violin concerto by Beethoven, Brahms, Mozart, or Tchaikovsky? Never, you say? Shame on you! Try it. Go to the library and check-out some classical music and fill your heart and brain with their organization, rhythm, meter and beauty. This kind of music edifies, it fills the soul and is beautiful, and is consistent in keeping the Sabbath day holy. Keep on listening until your spirit begins to respond positively to it. Many of the great composers, such as those above, have given credit to God for their inspirational music which often flooded their minds faster than they could write it down. But always remember that Satan has his own kind of music of hard rock and rap, which does not edify or fill the soul with goodness and beauty. Stay away from that kind of so-called music. It frankly is not good for you in any form.

You can also sing, and even sing in a group. Sing songs that give motivation to goodness. There are many country music and pop music songs which do such. You can also enjoy another person's company. You can take walks with family members and talk about spiritual concerns. You can watch a sunrise or sunset. You can visit the sick. You can observe nature. You can encourage others who are depressed or upset. You can comfort children and teach them good things. You can comfort the old people and listen and learn from them. You can also rest. *You can even communicate with one another at home.* Wow! That is such a novel idea. Imagine, actually taking some one-on-one time to really communicate with each other and getting to know each other's feelings on a variety of issues. You can do many things on the Sabbath day that can uplift and edify others, and in so doing, you only uplift and edify yourself.

5th Commandment

"Honour thy father and thy mother: that thy days may be long upon the land which the LORD thy God giveth thee." Exodus 20:12

Mary had always given her parents a hard time, especially her stepmother. Mary consistently broke her 11:00 p.m. curfew, she also rebelled against doing any of her chores around the house, she daily had sassy verbal exchanges with both parents, she fought with her brothers and sisters and generally was a great big major pain to everyone in the family. After an especially big argument where things were thrown about the house, Mary told her parents that she was moving out. Three days after she moved out, Mary's parents were killed in a car accident.

Mary was distraught. She could not be comforted. She cried for days. She could not even bring herself to attend the funeral, which greatly insulted the other family members. But Mary was feeling something that the other family members were not feeling. Mary was feeling great pangs of guilt. She now sorely regretted being such a constant major brat to her parents. Furthermore, because they were now dead, she could never tell them how sorry she was for all she had done to them and the rest of the family.

The remainder of Mary's life was dedicated to her parents. She eventually made up with the other family members. She put herself through the university where she became a counselor for troubled youth. She later wrote several books on the subject of troubled youth and became a noted lecturer. But it wasn't until later in her life that Mary finally received the forgiveness that she had sought for so long. It came during her nightly prayers. As she was asking for forgiveness for being such a dishonorable child to her parents, a still small voice came into her mind which gave her peace and told her that she was forgiven. The voice also told her to put the issue behind her and go forward with her work, for it was an important work and there were many people who would be strengthened by it.

Mary lived to be 90 years old. She never had to stay one day or night in a hospital. Her health had been quite wonderful. People who came to Mary's funeral commented that Mary's life seemed to be so happy and that it must have been because it was filled with so much unselfish service to others.

What do you think about Mary? Can people like the young Mary really turn their life around and become successful, caring people without their parents dying? The answer is "Yes." But does it take a major crises in order to turn a life around? No, but it unfortunately often does. However, there are many in this world who have turned their life around without a major crises, and you the reader, can also if you need and really want to. Desire is a key to success; you have to have the desire to turn your life around, for without the desire, nothing will likely happen. Had Mary's parents continued living, and had Mary continued to be such a dishonorable child, who knows what would have happened to Mary. She could have continued to be such a major pain to her parents that her life might have been shortened, because of it.

Upon the death of her parents, Mary had what psychologists call a Significant Emotional Event (S.E.E.), which helped turn her life around. After her parents were killed, which was a S.E.E., Mary went through a lot of self-introspection and what she found she did not like. (Maybe reading this book will be *your* S.E.E.). It was hard for Mary to forgive herself once she realized what kind of person she was. Furthermore, it was hard to get forgiveness from the source of all forgiveness, from Jesus Christ. But Mary persisted and became successful. Persistence is another key to success. *Never give up in your quest to become a better person.* It is my opinion that Mary's reunion with her parents in the next life will be a happy one. What do you think?

The Fifth Commandment is the only commandment in which there is a stated promise given to you if you keep the commandment. The promise is that your days will be long upon the land, which likely means you will be blessed with a longer life. *In other words, you will not be taken in death before your time on earth is supposed to end.* This is a great promise. How many people do you know who have died in their youth without being able to fulfill their dreams and aspirations, or the dreams and aspirations of their parents and loved ones? I believe that when people are obedient to the commandments, especially the Fifth Commandment, they are protected in ways that surpass understanding wherein accidents are prevented, diseases are averted, and life is preserved until that person's life is appointed unto death.

This does not necessarily mean that if someone dies as a youth, that he or she died before his or her time, nor does it mean that he or she did not honor his or her parents. It also does not necessarily mean that those who do not honor their parents will die young or that those who honor their parents will live until they are old. The commandment just states that if you honor your father and mother, your days will be long upon the land. Again, it means that you will not be taken before your allotted time here on earth is complete, and only God knows when that time is.

All of us as God's children here on earth need to be more willing to heed His will over our own will, and that includes the specific time that we are to leave this life for the next life. "But," you say, "what about those who do not necessarily want their days to be long upon the land?" Should they intentionally dishonor their parents in order to fulfill their own selfish wish? Silly question? Not so, especially in these days of assisted suicide. Regardless of how someone feels about the length of his or her life, he or she is still required to live the Fifth Commandment to honor both father and mother.

We mortals also have no business deciding when we or anyone else "should" die. However, this wouldn't apply if one's job is to carry out the verdict of a death sentence, and I am sympathetic for one who has such a job.

The decision as to when my or your life should end is really not mine or yours to make. This decision is to be made only by our Heavenly Father, or His son Jesus Christ. Although today, there unfortunately are many who consciously take their own life, and others who willingly assist others to die. It is a sad state of affairs we are in when suicide is presently the seventh leading cause of death in the United States and is reputed to be a "Yuppie" form of death. Statistics show that one out of 100 people attempt suicide at least once during his or her lifetime. People who commit suicide do not understand the seriousness of their deed as far as their eternal future is concerned. They also are often so selfish as to not even consider how devastating their suicide can be on those family members left behind. But what about those exceptions, who due to illness, disease, accidents or old age, have become a burden to those who care for them, especially family members? *Regardless of the situation,* we human beings are not to commit suicide, or even assist in the suicide of others. To do so will bring upon oneself the judgement of God, and it will not be good!

People who actually do commit suicide almost always precede the act with suicidal thoughts, verbal or written threats, statements and even half-hearted attempts at suicide. If you presently are thinking of suicide as a way out of your problems or sadness, get help immediately! Do it now, even before you continue reading.

What about those who are terminally ill? Should they be assisted in killing themselves? No, because killing is what it technically is, and we are commanded not to kill as indicated in the Sixth Commandment. It is as simple as that. However, there are many today who wrongly feel obligated to assist in suicides when asked to do so. Are these people trying to play the role of God? (I think they are, at least it appears to me that they are trying to play the role of God. And some of this is unfortunately being done with growing support for the effort from the medical community). I am not suggesting that terminally-ill patients should be given expensive treatment and procedures that are truly time consuming and useless. I just think that terminally-ill patients should be looked after, cared for and made comfortable until their time comes, but there should NOT be any active assistance in ending the patient's life any earlier than God's own timetable. This is even if the patient asks for assistance to end their own life. On the other hand, it should also be mentioned that overzealous, expensive and unnecessary treatments to purposefully extend the lives of obviously terminal patients should not be given or foisted upon the unsuspecting. This is especially so when the insurance coverage on the ill person becomes such a tempting target of unscrupulous medical people, and hopefully, there are but few of them.

Now, returning to the Fifth Commandment, what does it mean to actually honor your father and mother? It means to be obedient to your father and mother. It means that you respect them. If you feel that it is impossible with your particular kind of parents or situation, to respect their lifestyles or their choices, then it means that you must at least be respectful to them. It also means that you consider their advice and try to see it and use it in a positive sense. It means to live a life that does not cause pain and heartache to your parents, like the younger Mary did in the above case study. This is correct even though your parents may have given you a lot of pain and heartache. It means that you do not argue and fight with your parents, even though you may disagree with them. *Agree to disagree in an agreeable way.* It means you must forgive them if they have not been model parents, even as you might be asking them to forgive you for not being a model son or daughter. It means that you look out for the welfare of your parents. It means that you help them with chores around the house and with tasks that they might have trouble performing, especially with those chores and tasks that become more difficult as they get older. It means to honor the name they have given you and to do nothing to bring dishonor or ridicule upon them or the name they have given you. It means to appreciate the things they have done for you, the things they have given you and the time they have spent in taking care or providing for you. It means to appreciate, if nothing else, the very fact that they gave you life.

Your life may not presently be the best, but your life gives you opportunity for growth and change for the good. Be aware that you can change your life for the good and that you can make it a lot better. Also, remember that you could have been born in many other places of the world and at other times which were and presently are much worse than your present situation. *If your parents have done none of the above things very well, you are still required to live the Fifth Commandment and to do your very best until you finally can forgive, appreciate and love them. It is your responsibility as a son or stepson, or a daughter or stepdaughter, to do so.* Nothing less is really acceptable. Once you do faithfully live the Fifth Commandment, you are taking upon yourself godly characteristics.

Regardless of the failings of our parents, you and I are still required to honor them in the ways suggested above, as well as in many other ways which are not necessarily suggested above. Within your own family, you probably know what the best ways are to honor your mother and father. If you don't know, then get the courage to ask them. If they are still alive, talk to them, even if you have to first ask for their forgiveness for your own shortcomings to them, regardless of their own shortcomings. At the very least, *talk to them*. Ask them about their own life experiences. Tell them you appreciate and love them for what they have done for you, even if it is so very little, and then ask what they require from you to honor them. You might be in for quite a shock when they give you their honest answer. (I believe that parents are often much more forgiving than most sons and daughters are of their parents). Parents are usually more forgiving than sons and daughters will ever suppose them to be. That is until those sons and daughters become parents themselves. Then they will begin to understand what forgiveness is all about, especially when their own children grow up to be rebellious teenagers!

To honor your parents also means that you are to take care of them as they get older. The United States of America has more homes for the elderly per capita than any other developed country. I feel that generally, we as Americans give less respect and honor to our elders than all the other developed countries. We have a tendency to ship them off to the retirement or nursing home sometimes long before it is necessary. I have seen it in families time and time again. Maybe it is because of the aggressive marketing strategies that many retirement and nursing homes use. And yet, I know that taking care of elderly parents or grandparents who cannot care for themselves can be a very taxing and difficult task. So don't feel quite so guilty if this is your situation. You have probably done the right thing if you have put them in a good care facility, but remember to visit them and treat them special as often as you can (see the movie "Driving Miss Daisy." Therein you will see that constant love and devotion can change even very cranky old people).

On the other hand, it could be that since both parents work in most American families, there is no one at home or there are not enough appropriate facilities at home to take care of elderly parents or grandparents. This is the more likely scenario than American families just turning away from their elderly parents or grandparents, at least I hope it is!

However, there are many other countries and societies who more effectively honor their elders than Americans do through seeking their wisdom and experience from the past, having them participate in new enterprises and seeking their direction in many new efforts dedicated to the future. It is only recently, relatively speaking, that some groups like the liberal American Association of Retired People (A.A.R.P.) and conservative groups like the Assoication of Mature American Citizens (A.M.A.C.) have come to have some clout in a variety of national and local issues. But this clout has only come as a result of frustration on the part of older retired people for not previously having a collective voice in anything. It did not come as a result of the good-nature of younger people wanting their elders to have more visibility and input into the present world.

I love it when I see the bumper sticker on an expensive camper or mobile home which says, "We are spending our children's inheritance." The older folks are honestly telling us something that we younger generation should listen carefully to! But then, I will soon be a part, albeit, an active part of that "older generation." It is an interesting experience to grow older, not fun, but truly interesting.

Today, many young people, and not-so-young people, delay leaving home to start their own families due to a variety of reasons, which are usually economic. They often have not prepared themselves well for the future, but the future is now! And the parents, and even grandparents, more often than not, are continuing to pay their older children and grandchildrens' expenses with no relief in sight. In a lot of so-called "less sophisticated societies," the situation is reversed. The children, fondly, look after and take care of their parents, especially as they get older. Today in America, there are many grandparents who are raising their own children's children. *Thank goodness for not only good parents, but for good grandparents as well!*

There are many youth today who have not a clue as to what the "real world" is really about, let alone knowing about honoring their parents. They have often not been individually or even collectively prepared properly to care for themselves, let alone care for anyone else, through proper job or skill preparation. They often slide through school as if it were a joke. In truth, it really is a joke, but unfortunately the joke is on them! And yet these people so often marry young people who are just as unprepared for married life and for the future as they are. How then can such a grossly unprepared grown adult child honor his or her parents by continuing to be a totally dependent burden upon them for basic sustenance? I think it is a difficult task and is a terribly unfair thing to ask especially of grandparents. However, I have seen it done and it sometimes has been done well. Again, thank goodness for merciful parents and grandparents, for there are many youth who would be totally lost without them.

I have observed both older children and grandchildren who have had major setbacks in life, wherein they had to depend upon their parents or grandparents for everyday help. In fact, I am a case in point. My parents as well as my in-laws, from both marriages, have helped when things got tough, especially in financial things. I am not a wealthy man, and I have thus, appreciated their help, and verbally expressed it to them.

On the other hand, I have seen children and grandchildren not only express and display thankfulness to their parents and grandparents who have helped them, they have also honored them in many ways. (I have tried to do similar). These children and grandchildren have helped their parents or grandparents by taking care of them when they could not care for themselves. They shopped for them, they fed them, they talked with them, they read to them, they prayed with and for them, they bathed them, they clothed them, they loved them and they made them feel special and important. *Thank goodness for thankful children and thankful grandchildren.*

If you are one of those wonderful children or grandchildren, as described above, may God bless you in every way. However, if you are one of those "young or not so young unprepared people," or even one of those unthankful young people, also as described above, start today to make something of yourself. First, talk with your parents, maybe for the first time in a long time, about what you should do to obtain good job skills, life skills, education or training to be able to exist and be productive on your own. Get their suggestions and possibly their support for you to make something of yourself. Do it today! If your parents can't help you, then seek other ways to improve yourself. See your religious leaders for advice or other honorable people in your community whom you respect. In any case, you will thus honor your parents and society as well by doing so.

6th Commandment

"Thou shalt not kill." Exodus 20:13

Del and Myrtle had been going with each other for about two years when Myrtle found out she was pregnant. After three months of arguing with Del, she finally gave in and had an abortion. The fetus was a baby girl.

Shortly thereafter, Myrtle began having second thoughts about her abortion. She soon became depressed and started taking drugs. She started having bad dreams about the baby. Things continued to worsen until Myrtle took her own life with a drug overdose.

Del heard about Myrtle's suicide and went berserk. In his anger he beat an old man to death. Because of how brutal the beating was, Del was booked on the charge of first degree murder.

In the above case study, how many times do you think the Sixth Commandment was broken? Read it again, and then make your guess. There were three killings, but the commandment was actually broken four times. Both Myrtle and Del will have to answer for the abortion, which ended the life of the little girl to be, Myrtle will also have to answer for her own suicide and Del will then have to answer for his murdering the old man. When one is responsible for taking a human life, *including their own*, he or she will be held accountable. It might not take place in this world, but one can be very sure it will take place at the Judgement Bar of God.

For the three individuals above, do you think there are any mitigating circumstances which might reduce the severity of their sins? There may be, especially in the case of Myrtle. But Del's situation looks pretty grim, not only from an earthly standpoint, but more importantly, from an eternal one as well.

In any case, killing is a terrible sin. Murder is even worse, because it usually involves premeditation or willful thinking and planning. Don't ever commit either of these two extremely serious sins. If you already have, then you must live the best life you can from now on, doing good unto all for the rest of your life, and then hope for the best in the eternities to come. Now, continue with instruction on the Sixth Commandment.

What does it mean to "not Kill?" There are thousands of cows, chickens, fish and other animals, as well as plants that are killed every day to help feed mankind. Are those who kill these animals and plants guilty of breaking the Sixth Commandment? No, they are not. In Genesis Chapter 1 verse 28, it says:

> ***"And God blessed them, and God said unto them (Adam and Eve), Be fruitful and multiply, and replenish the earth, and subdue it: and have dominion over the fish of the sea, and over the fowl of the air, and over every living thing that moveth upon the earth."***

Adam and Eve and their descendants were commanded to have dominion over the animals and plants of the earth. In verses 29 and 30 of Genesis Chapter 1, it is further stated that animals and green herbs are given by God as meat for man. These commandments by no means give mankind the permission to wantonly kill animals and even plants for pleasure, sport or wealth. Those who do such activities will have to answer to God someday for these gross deeds. In this situation, I feel of even greater concern however, is the extreme display of selfishness when wantonly killing animals for sport or wealth. This kind of personal selfishness will likely be manifest unfortunately in other ways throughout a person's life which will be more serious and usually results in more serious consequences. In addition, any youth that wantonly and viciously kills animals, immediately needs psychological and spiritual help before they start killing human beings. If you know of a youth in this situation, do not hesitate to do something positive about it. Report it to someone who can be of help to him or her.

The author feels the real intent of the Sixth Commandment is that we should not kill human beings, not just other human beings, but *any* human beings, which includes ourselves. In both the Old Testament and in the New Testament, we are commanded to not kill. In Leviticus 24:17 and 21 it states:

> ***"And he that killeth any man shall surely be put to death."***
> ***"And he that killeth a beast, he shall restore it: and he that killeth a man, he shall be put to death."***

The above scripture indicates that if one were to kill a beast (a lamb, a camel, a horse, etc.) that he or she needs to restore or replace it with another like unto the one which was killed. However, when one kills another human being, there is not possible restoration or replacement. This is partly why the killing of human beings is such a serious sin.

But what about those who kill in war? Will they be held accountable to the same standard as one who premeditates before he or she kills or murders someone? The recent war in Vietnam, in which the author participated, provides a good platform for discussion. And as a participant over there, although I personally knew of only one who was a genuine murder suspect, I am quite sure that there were premeditated murders committed under the disguise of war and done for personal gain. Those who did such things, and who yet still do them, will receive their just reward in the next life, even if no one on earth, other than themselves, know about their terrible actions. *Be assured, the sin of killing another human being will be accounted for.*

On the other hand, there were also many killings committed by young men who were either protecting themselves, their fellow soldiers or in some way protecting their own country. The author believes that at the Judgement Day we will all be judged by what was in our heart and mind which really caused us to do some of the crazy things we do in this life, including killing. I believe that those who have had to kill in war in order to preserve self, and others, as well as their country and way of life, will not be accountable for killing under the Sixth Commandment. There are no references in the Bible to specifically support the author's argument. However, there have been many people killed, by the hands of the "chosen" people in the Bible, in wars fought after the original Ten Commandments were received. Never is it mentioned in the scriptures that those who killed in war will be held accountable and judged against the Sixth Commandment. And this seems to be regardless of whether one was fighting on the side of the Lord or on the other side! It should be remembered however, that war is not and never will be an acceptable excuse for wanton killing, especially murder. Murder shows the devilish intent and ultimate selfishness of the heart of the person who murders.

To continue with the original discussion, the punishment for killing in the Old Testament was death, and usually by stoning (see Matthew 23:37, John 8:7, 8:59, 10:31-32 and 11:8). There were no such things as firing squads, guillotines or mercy drugs as there are today.

In Matthew, Chapter 5 verse 21, it is stated:

"Ye have heard that it was said by them of old time, Thou shalt not kill; and whosoever shall kill shall be in danger of the judgement."

The above verse is part of the Sermon on the Mount that Jesus preached. If there had been any change in the deathly punishment for killing, as was the practice in the Old Testament, this would have been the most appropriate place for it to be explained. But no, the Savior states that those who kill will be in danger of the judgement of God, not "might" be, but "will" be!

In Mark 10:19, the Savior addresses five of the Ten Commandments, including the commandment to not kill. The reader *should not think even for one moment* that because the First, Second, Third, Fourth and Tenth Commandments were not mentioned, that Jesus Christ was doing away with them. In fact, in the above verse, He included to "Defraud not," or in other words, to not cheat, which is something beyond bearing false witness or lying. Thus, is "Defraud not," a new commandment? Well, it certainly seems to be when offered by Jesus Christ, and I would live it as best I can. Also, to not defraud someone has to do with honesty and integrity, and one who is completely honest will not lie, steal, cheat, covet or defraud. Suffice it to say, make sure you are consistent with the spirit of the law and not be so foolish as to start counting to see if the Savior *secretly* deleted or added to the original Ten Commandments, *for he did neither.* He did however, later in the New Testament, command us in many ways and He also gave us the Two Great Commandments, which will be addressed later in the book.

You and I are to live all the commandments, and as we both progress through life and as you progress through this book, we both will hopefully learn to live a godly life. In so doing, all of the commandments will become second nature to you, for because of your increased love for Heavenly Father and Jesus Christ, your behavior will be living in full accordance with all the commandments and will want to do nothing less.

In Galatians 5:21 and 1st John 3:15 we read where those who murder will not inherit the Kingdom of God nor will they have eternal life. This means that those who murder another human being, will not be able to go with nor live with Heavenly Father and His son Jesus Christ. Yet, they will be resurrected in the third resurrection of the wicked and will still live forever. But because of their wickedness on earth, they must suffer the "second death," which is to live forever without the presence of the Father and the Son. What a terrible fate to wait for and wonder about. Those who wilfully murder will eventually wish they never had been born. Again, wanton killing or murder is the ultimate act of human selfishness.

To not kill or murder also means that *we should not kill ourselves as well as not kill other human beings.* To kill oneself is like unto killing another person, and again, the scriptures are very clear as to what should be done to one who kills (see Genesis 9:6, and Leviticus 24:17 and 21).

It is interesting that there are no similar statements or deathly conditions in the New Testament as in the Old Testament scriptures above, as to what to do with killers or murderers. However, there is with at least one exception. In Revelations 13:10, it is stated that when one kills by the sword, he (or she) must die by the sword. This condition of scant support in the New Testament for the "death penalty," may have helped the cause of those today who literally fight to stop all capital executions from being carried out. It should be remembered however, that the prophets and the writers of the New Testament books were true believers in the basic true teachings of the Old Testament, such as faith, repentance, baptism, the gift of the Holy Ghost and the Ten Commandments, for they lived them and they taught them. As a result they could have possibly not felt the need to emphasize commandment punishments which were so universally known and generally accepted by the people, and the "death penalty" for murder was one of them.

On the other hand, support for only imprisonment for murder in the New Testament is almost nil, and the two verses which could support it are at best, a big stretch. The only verses, after a long search, are found in Luke 23:18-19. And these verses only tell that Barabbas, a murderer, was cast into prison. There is nothing written to indicate that Barabbas was to stay permanently in prison or that he was just awaiting his death sentence, which is the more likely situation. In any case, we know that Barabbas was released upon demand of the chief Jewish priests, rulers and people, and that Jesus Christ then took his place. Jesus Christ was shortly thereafter crucified on Golgotha.

In the previous discussion on the Fifth Commandment, it was pointed out that suicide was presently the seventh leading cause of death in the U.S. That is a lot of people killing themselves! What a sad state of affairs we have gotten ourselves into. The really unfortunate thing is that it has been and is still being done by individual choice. The killing of human beings in any form is a most serious sin and should be avoided at all costs.

Those who kill or have assistance in killing themselves, do not understand that our bodies are not ours until after the Resurrection. Until that time, our bodies are owned by Jesus Christ. Remember, He paid for each of us by shedding His blood in Gethsemane and then dying on the cross on Golgotha. *We have no authority nor any right to take either someone else's life or our own life, regardless of the physical pain or discomfort being experienced.* When it is our time to go, we will be taken and we should not be taken even one day sooner. The author thinks that one who takes his or her own life may not be dealt with quite like a willful murderer will be. None-the-less, it is a serious enough sin that no one in his or her right mind should ever even think about it, let alone actually do it. Suicide is an ultimately self-serving and very selfish act, that often has devasting consequences on those left behind. You are again reminded as in the Fifth Commandment section, if you have any thoughts of suicide for whatever reason or reasons, get help today.

Those who seek assistance to have their own lives ended are really no different from those who shoot or poison themselves. If anyone tries to talk you into helping them end their life prematurely, try to talk them out of of it and let nature take its own course. If you have personally thought about asking someone to assist you in ending your life, then seek professional help immediately. Take courage and pray to your Heavenly Father for help. Put your life in His hands, not in the hands of someone to assist you to die. Talk to either a professional counselor or a religious leader or call the suicide hot-line nearest your location. *Do something about it now, before you even continue reading this book!*

How does the Sixth Commandment apply to those who elect to have abortions, especially abortions of convenience or abortions due to just not wanting to have a baby, such as in the case study? *Only legally speaking,* abortion might not be quite as bad a sin as premeditated murder, because of the very earthly undecided legal status of the unborn fetus. However, do not take any comfort in the above statement, because abortion for any reason means the willful termination of a human life. Termination of a human life by another willing human being is an extremely serious sin, especially when it is willfully done. I personally would not want to have anything to do with any part of any abortion.

Those who take part in abortions where no rape or incest has been committed or where the life of the woman is not at stake, will all have to answer for this terrible sin someday. This applies to the man who suggests the abortion, the woman who agrees to have the abortion or the physician, medical people or anyone who willingly assists in the abortion or even the person who willing drives the "patient" to the abortion site. You can bet your farm on it! However, it again probably will not be in this world as wickedness generally seems to be prevailing over righteousness, but it will be in the next life where people will learn just how horrible their abortion deeds have been. If you or your friends are presently considering an abortion, *please seek help* from your Heavenly Father through real dedicated prayer. *Remember, remember, oh remember that your Father in Heaven does not want you to have an abortion!* But also remember, that Satan does want you to have an abortion, because it destroys life, and the destruction of life is not limited only to the little ones who are deprived of birth. I really believe that anyone associated with willful and unnecessary abortions will die a little bit at a time, until if unchecked, will become without feeling or sensitivity to life and death itself. Your dedicated personal prayers will be answered in your receiving strength to resist the temptation to have an abortion. Sincerely pray for some alternatives and then prayerfully select one. Be aware that there are many who patiently await the opportunity to adopt babies. Your selfless act of giving up the baby for adoption through an authorized agency will be a great blessing to others, and will save the baby from a terrible death! Above all, don't give in to Satan, especially on this important subject.

Women who have had abortions of convenience or who just did not want to have the baby, and who are honest about revealing their feelings, usually feel a great loss for the rest of their life. Also, they usually go through the emotional stages of grief and mourning, such as a person who lost their spouse or child to death. There is also much remorse for women and often quiet wonderment as to how serious a sin their abortion actually is. In addition, the men who have demanded or even encouraged their wives or girlfriends to have abortions, often terribly regret their selfish decisions as they grow older and maybe somewhat wiser, and more repentant. Unfortunately for them all, *abortion is a very serious sin because there is no one in this world who can give life back once it has been taken.* This is true whether the life is an unborn yet still live fetus, or a little girl, or a little boy, or a teenager, or a parent or grandparent. Of course, there are those women and men who are beyond care and feeling, and could care less about whether or not there was any sin committed through abortion. In their minds they have unfortunately rationalized their great sin away. Even medical people have done this. They have truly gone beyond feeling. However, they will have their time at the Judgement Day and it will not be a pleasant time for them. The author would not want to be in their shoes for any amount of money or any earthly possession.

If you have been a part of any abortion and you sincerely feel terrible about it, and well you should, you need to seek help and forgiveness. The help can come from a variety of public and private sources, as well as from church groups and professionals. However, in order to get forgiveness you must get on your knees and ask forgiveness from God our Heavenly Father, in the name of Jesus Christ, and *this must be a serious and an ongoing effort because it will not be easy and not immediate.* If the forgiveness eventually comes to you, and it is possible that it can, consider yourself to be extremely fortunate and blessed. In almost all cases, abortion is a sin in which mankind does not have the power to provide the ultimate forgiveness, regardless of how much penance or how many "Hail Mary's," or whatever one is directed to say or do. Also, forgiveness of this sin is not just an easy one-shot thing. Abortions are serious enough sins that it will take a lot of time sincerely repenting, fasting, praying and basically changing one's self in order to receive your forgiveness, and only God or Jesus Christ can ultimately give it to you. Your repentance needs to be extended to your parents whom you may have injured, the other person involved and his or her parents and anyone else close to you whom you may have offended. And how do you repent to the little one whose life you have terminated? Well, maybe we will find out in the life to come, and that is a scary thought. Remember, that none of these people can actually forgive you for the act of abortion, but they can forgive you personally, thus enabling you to go on with your life. Again remember, only God or Jesus Christ can give you the ultimate forgiveness you need to be truly clean from the act of abortion.

Why is it that people kill? Other than premeditated murder, which is actually only a small percent of the total number of killings committed, most murders or killings are committed out of passion, jealousy, anger or complete stupidity. The drive-by shootings, the domestic disputes, the killing of crying babies, are usually the result of uncontrolled anger, stupidity or the lack of self-control. Children of today do not know how to control or properly vent their anger when it enrages them. The author feels this is because, in most instances, they have not had a parent or adult instrumental in their life who has been able to provide them with self-control skills sufficient to control their own anger. I have two wonderful daughters and three wonderful sons, one of which had a terrible uncontrollable temper as a child. In working, teaching and through good example training, the young man learned to control his anger. He has since been in good control of all his emotions and has turned out to be a really neat young man because of it.

There are many children today who live with adults who themselves haven't a clue as to how to control their own emotions, especially their own anger. Is there any wonder why children of today can not control their anger? Anger is such a destructive force that most people really do not know how to deal with it when they come face to face with it.

One of the best ways to control anger, especially in classroom settings is a technique called "Timeout." This is where a person, usually a troublesome student, is removed from the "trigger situation" which initially caused the anger. When dealing with adults, it is often impossible to remove them from the "trigger situation." Thus, adults as well as older teenagers either have to learn how to control their own anger, or learn how to deal with the probable very negative consequences of their uncontrolled anger. The resultant consequence may be life imprisonment or even death. Without getting into any actual behavioral therapy, which goes beyond the scope of this book, there are three simple techniques which can be of immense help to people who can not control their anger.

The first technique is one that has been mentioned earlier in this book and in the workbook. The technique can also work in helping you to control your anger. It is a form of aversion therapy. It simply involves you wearing a stout but lose rubber band around your wrist and flipping yourself whenever you feel yourself getting angry. You may have to flip yourself sharply more than once in order to remind yourself of what you are trying to do. And of course, you are trying to keep anger from getting the best of you and having it control what you do and say.

The second technique for anger control is a form of the "Timeout" technique described above. It simply involves you concentrating and slowly counting to ten when you feel real anger coming on. By putting your mind on something other than anger, you can delay and thus reduce your anger until it is controllable.

The third technique involves taking a deep breath and then slowly exhaling. While exhaling, you concentrate to keep your emotions on the bottom side of the exhale. Again, by delaying your anger, you can eventually get control of it.

If there is someone taunting you, then if you can, remove yourself from the situation immediately while slowly doing your count or your exhaling. If anger is thrown at you by others, move away a few inches or feet to the side and let it pass by you. Don't let it hit you. Also, if you are about to strike someone or you are about to yell and scream at someone, stop yourself, then concentrate and start slowly counting to ten or taking a deep breath and slowly exhaling.

Real uncontrollable anger can come and quickly go, thus if you have a plan such as is being explained to you, the next time anger grabs hold of you, put your plan into action and set your mind to counting and most likely when you have reached the slow count to ten, the uncontrollable anger will be gone. If it isn't, then do another count, and then keep counting or keep breathing deeply and slowly exhaling until you cool off.

If the people who find they have real problems with anger would take time to plan ahead to implement any or all of the above techniques, they would find they can much better control their emotional lives. *One who is always in control of his or her emotions, is almost always in control of their behavior.* Of course, if alcohol or drugs are a part of the picture, then the anger is much less likely to be controlled. The partaking of alcohol and drugs is part of the stupidity that was mentioned earlier. And Satan loves you to be stupid, because you will do as he wants you to do when you partake of alcohol and drugs, regardless of your station or position in life! Needless-to-say, *get rid of your alcohol and drugs before they carefully lead you down to the most terrible part of real Hell and eternal misery.*

If you have behaviorial problems with anger, practice the three techniques above. If in addition to your anger, you take drugs, are hooked on caffeine, you smoke, you chew, you have problems with sex, you overeat and are susceptible to drinking alcohol, then I suggest that you take care of these problems first. Enroll yourself into a 10 or 12 step personal improvement program and faithfully attend on a daily or weekly basis. If you haven't already, faithfully attend an Alcoholic's Anonymous or similar type of program. You will be impressed regardless of your own problems. I believe the Alcoholic's Anonymous program has helped improve the lives of more individuals with significant problems than any other secular program and better than most religous programs.

The more you especially do drugs and alcohol, the less able you are to control your temper, or anything else. *But, you be a real man, or a real woman. Take charge of your life. Don't let anything like drugs, food, tobacco, alcohol, sex or anything else control you. You must control them first before you can effectively control your own anger.* If you need professional help, get it now. Do not delay. There usually are several help organizations who can help you recover from your addictions. Look in the Yellow Pages. Alcoholics Anonymous is listed there, as are several other lunch oriented organizations. These organizations can be of great help to you. Take courage. *Do something today about it. Do it now, even before continuing to the next commandment!*

7th Commandment

"Thou shalt not commit adultery." Exodus 20:14

Rose was as pretty as her name. She had everything — beauty, charm, intelligence, personality, and money were all part of the package. However, Rose liked to flirt with the boys. Even after she married the most handsome and capable guy in school, she still liked to flirt. Her flirting at the office where she worked was often viewed as being cute. But as it continued over the years, Rose would get herself into some difficult situations.

Recently, a new, rugged-looking man came to work as a temporary in the office. Rose sought him out as a challenge. *As one small thing led to another*, she soon found herself in bed with him. The next day she felt so bad about herself that she confided in one of her trusted office workers. But the temptation was too much for the "trusted friend," for soon everyone in the office knew about Rose and the new rugged office worker. Rose's husband soon found out and immediately filed for divorce. Although they sought counseling to stave off the divorce, Rose's husband said that the problem was not his, and refused to attend the counseling sessions. The divorce went forward to completion. Rose lost her family because her now ex-husband did a good job of turning the children against her. Rose also lost her job since no one in the office would trust her anymore. And, of course, the rugged temporary office worker had long gone.

Rose lost everything. Now as she approached middle age she realized she no longer was a young beauty, and the toll of all her experiences had put a major damper on her once bubbly personality. Unless she gets help from some organization, family or friends, Rose is going to find that under the present circumstances, life can be very hard and cruel. But then, she must face the consequence of her own decisions, as all of us must do.

A major part of an individual's life is that of bearing the consequences of decisions one makes. Good decisions usually lead to good consequences, and conversely, bad decisions usually lead to bad consequences. This is a universal principle of behavior. It is too bad that most people do not learn this simple principle. Thus, if one really desires to have a happy life, his or her chances of having it are significantly better when he or she makes good decisions.

The above case study on adultery could have easily been based around a man rather than a woman, which seems to be the more frequent occurrence. However, in either situation, the point illustrated by the case study is that adultery hits the other spouse right in the heart like nothing else can. The lack of self-control, the betrayal, the lack of trust, the lack of faith are all devastating to the other spouse. Many people can not successfully overcome adultery in a marriage. To overcome adultery by either spouse, takes great strength, faith, understanding, dedication and love. But these are characteristics in which most people today are sorely lacking.

If you are married and are especially attracted to someone of the opposite sex, other than your spouse, discuss it delicately with your spouse. Immediately get your spouse's help and suggestions. Or, if you are quite sure that discussion with your spouse would only hurt the situation, then you *must become proactive* on your own to save your marriage. Renew your marriage commitment to your spouse. Take a romantic vacation with your spouse, even if it is only for a couple of days. Seek counseling together with a good, religious-oriented counselor. Put some fun back into your marriage by better meeting the needs of your spouse, by taking walks and by actually communicating with each other. And especially, if at all possible, remove yourself from talking or even meeting with the other tempting person, and *never* meet alone with he or she. Further, be proactive in preventing any possible adulterous situation. Don't trade possible eternal happiness for a short time of unauthorized physical pleasure. You will really regret it if you do.

The author was told a cute joke years ago and it seems quite appropriate to present. It seems that a man was fed up with his wife and marriage, and thus wanted a divorce. He evidently had a big argument with his wife and as a result, was still very angry. He sought out his good friend, who was a marriage counselor, to give him some good advice on how he could really hurt his wife emotionally before telling her about the divorce. Of course, this put the marriage counselor in a bad situation, because he wanted to help his friend but also save his marriage at the same time. After much thought and prayer, the counselor later told his friend that the best way to emotionally hurt his wife would be to treat her like a queen for two weeks. He was counseled to love her, to give her gifts, to praise her, to express feelings of tenderness to her, to do some of the house work and to generally treat her as if she were something very special for two weeks! Following the two weeks, the friend was told to bring her a box of candy with some flowers and then soon after tell her about the divorce and then tell her he never wanted to see her again. It was agreed that this would really break her heart. The man went away anxious to implement this ingenious plan on the very next day.

The counselor did not see his friend for over six months. When the counselor finally did see him, his friend was with some beautiful lady in a nice restaurant. The counselor, thinking the man had evidently divorced his wife and picked up this new lady, approached the man and lady at their table. Following his brief introduction, he carefully asked his friend how the plan went. The man's eyes lit up and he responded, "Doc, your advice was the best advice I have ever had." Gesturing to the beautiful lady, the man said, "I want you to meet my wonderful one-and-only wife." "She is my queen, she is the light of my life, she is everything good about me." "She is the best thing about me, and to think that I about lost her." "Thanks Doc for all your help, you really did save our marriage."

The real message from the above story is that when we *consistently* treat people, especially our spouse, as if they really are special, they seem as if by magic to be transformed into the special and wonderful person we first married. Of course, the change that takes place does so not only in both people but especially in the eye of the beholder. *It is important to remember that the simple act of giving praise, rather than criticism, can significantly change both people for the better.* It is so simple to do yet happens so seldom in even our own families.

If your present marriage is not good, and you have taken several positive steps to save it, such as those mentioned above, but to no avail, still do not end it with an adulterous affair. End it in an amicable way through an honorable divorce, and there are such things. Adultery is *not* a way that any thinking or caring person would use to get back at a spouse. Adultery is a serious sin and it always hurts all parties involved, especially children.

For your own happiness, stay away from adultery. Stay away from even the temptation of adultery, for it has an enticing but potentially deadly consequence. Treat the temptation of adultery as if it were a poisonous snake, for it is as dangerous.

Over the years the Seventh Commandment is one that seems to have undergone a significant change in its interpretation or possibly it's perceived interpretation of unimportance. For today, adultery in most of the states within America is not even important enough or reason enough for divorcement, as it once was. Today, people who commit adultery seem to be more worried about being caught and embarrassed, or having their spouse find out with resultant financial consequences. Potential adulterers would be best advised to worry about the long-term earthly consequences but especially the eternal consequences of breaking the Seventh Commandment.

For those who do not officially know what adultery is, the Webster's New World Dictionary, 1996 edition, states that adultery is:

"Voluntary sexual intercourse between a married man and a woman not his wife, or between a married woman and a man not her husband: see also fornication".

For those who do not officially know what fornication is, the Webster's New World Dictionary, 1996 edition, states that fornication is:

"Voluntary sexual intercourse engaged in by a man, especially an unmarried man, with an unmarried woman: or voluntary

sexual intercourse engaged in by an unmarried person: if the other person is married, the act of the unmarried person is sometimes also considered adultery".

The act of fornication, as stated above, is like unto adultery. Thus, those who practice it are in danger of the same judgement that those who commit adultery will receive. This is regardless of what laws man has either made or done away with concerning adultery. And for those interested, man's modern-day law defines sexual intercourse as penetration, however slight.

In Corinthians 6:18-20, the Apostle Paul taught baptized church members to:

"Flee fornication. Every sin that a man doeth is without the body; but he that committeth fornication sinneth against his own body. What? know ye not that your body is the temple of the Holy Ghost which is in you, which ye have of God, and ye are not your own? For ye are bought with a price; therefore glorify God in your body, and in your spirit, which are God's."

Fornication and adultery are serious sins. When we sin against ourselves, we sin against our body and spirit which are only on loan to us from Jesus Christ, until the Resurrection. Treat your body and spirit with great respect and they will both treat you well in return.

I have recently reviewed some unpublished data on a few hundred men and women which was not too scientifically gathered, but none-the-less, the data strongly indicated that 100% of those who engaged in extramarital sex while married, had also previously engaged in sex before marriage. *This data suggests that those who do not control their sexual urges before marriage do not learn to control these urges even after marriage, and thus are more susceptible to dangerous and sinful extramarital affairs.* Certainly, more research and data are needed to confirm this scary correlation, because correlations don't accurately prove cause and effect. As a corollary however, it has always been my opinion that those who gain control over their sexual urges before marriage will have greater control of those urges after marriage, thus protecting the marriage from extramarital affairs.

Those who practice other sexual activities such as oral sex, heavy petting or homosexual behavior in lieu of sexual intercourse outside of an authorized marriage commitment between a man and a woman, are also in danger of the same judgement as unrepentant adulterers. Sexual infidelity and deviant sexual behavior in any form are two of the biggest problems that we have in the world today, and the problems seem to be getting worse. If you have any of the above problems, get help or counseling immediately! Do not delay this most important action. Do something about it today! There are competent sex therapists who can be contacted from the Yellow Pages.

When Jehovah gave Moses the Ten Commandments, He gave them with an overall descending order of commandment importance by listing the most important ones first and then on to the last ones. This evidently was done through three main groupings of the commandments. (There will be more about this in the "In Summary" section of the book). This should not however, denigrate or reduce in any way the importance of the last five commandments to the mind and heart of the reader. The

Seventh Commandment to not commit adultery, either by itself, or in conjunction with all the other commandments, is very important to keep. *Moral fidelity and sexual purity in and out of marriage should be kept at all costs,* but if unfortunately lost, the person or persons must sincerely repent and never repeat the offense or similar offenses ever again.

Throughout the Old Testament, as well as in the New Testament, the breaking of any of the original Ten Commandments, usually brought about severe consequences. This was especially so for the four commandments to not kill, to not commit adultery, to not blaspheme or say the name of God in vain, and the commandment to keep the Sabbath day holy. The consequence was almost always death for the guilty party. The breaker of especially these four commandments, since they were and still are so easily observable when broken, would lose his or her life, usually by being stoned to death (see Leviticus 20:10-21, 24:10-23, Numbers 15:32-35, Proverbs 6:32-33 and John 8:7). In the New Testament it is clearly pointed out that *unrepentant adulterers along with other wicked people will suffer the judgments of God in the next world and will not inherit the Kingdom of God* (see Hebrews 13:4, Revelations 21:8, 22:14-15, 1st Corinthians 6:9-10). This means that eternal life with Heavenly Father and Jesus Christ will not be available to these unrepentant people.

It is interesting to note that the Bible scriptures often do not distinguish between married persons and unmarried persons when the sin of adultery is mentioned. Also, the sin of fornication, as discussed above, is usually associated directly with the sin of adultery. Thus again, those who fornicate before marriage may be close to experiencing similar future judgements as those who commit adultery after they have married (see 1st Corinthians 6:9-20)!

We could assume from the Bible that since the above four commandments seem to be more visible, dramatic in their breaking and more directly prove the lack of integrity of a person, they are mentioned more often with their terminal consequences than are the other commandments. Being such, they likely are more difficult to receive forgiveness from when broken. This is true, and especially so when adultery and killing are concerned. When you commit adultery you cannot easily restore the destroyed trust that you once committed to uphold nor restore the virtue which may have also been taken. When you kill you cannot *ever* restore the life you have taken. It is the same for virtue. How can you repent when part of the repentance process is to restore, as much as possible, that which was destroyed or taken away? This is why man cannot give true forgiveness especially to those who murder, kill or take away virtue. Only God our Father in Heaven or Jesus Christ can give the appropriate forgiveness, but you should not take great comfort in getting it, because killing, or particularly premeditated murder, is such a serious and grievous sin. However, as stated similarly in a previous section, if you have committed adultery or even murder, never do either again. Do much good the rest of your life, pray, fast, repent and hope for the best now and in the world to come.

Although committing murder or killing in today's society are considered to be much more serious crimes than adultery, the scriptures tell a different story. This has been clearly indicated in the biblical references provided above. It seems to the author that to sacrifice eternal life and living with our Heavenly Father and His son Jesus Christ because of committing adultery *and not sincerely repenting of it*, is a personal loss of monumental proportions with unfortunate eternal consequences. To the author, the real "Hell" the scriptures describe is to lose out on having eternal life with Heavenly Father and His son Jesus Christ. And I think that when the *unrepentant* adulterer finally realizes all that Jesus Christ has personally done for every person, he or she will eternally regret their adultry. This will be compounded when each person becomes aware of what our Father in Heaven has prepared for those who love Him and who demonstrate that love by their being worthy *commandment keepers*.

Eternity is a long time. We need to work very hard in this life in preparing ourselves to be worthy for life in the eternities. *We need to individually prove that we can live a righteous life while still on the earth*. In fact, this is what life on earth is for, to prove to God that we can become worthy a little bit at a time. And certainly, repentance should be a very real part of every person's life. Repentance should make good men and women out of bad men and women, and make even better men and women out of already good men and women! Repentance can truly make godly like people.

So, now that the argument is pretty strong against adultery, and adulterers. If you are guilty of breaking the Seventh Commandment, do not shun repentance and remain unclean. If you truly want to repent, and you should, what can you do and how can you do it? Probably the best approach is again, as in breaking any of the commandments, to get on your knees first, to confess your sins and seek heavenly help through real dedicated prayer and fasting. Do not just offer one prayer, *but many, and make them as sincere as possible. Due to the seriousness of the sin, forgiveness will not come to you easily, and it won't come quickly. You can depend on this! But, if you are sincere and do not return to your adultery, if you work very hard at becoming a much better person, and you confess your sins to God and make appropriate confessions and amends to those you have injured, your forgiveness will eventually come.* You will know it in your heart when it comes.

You also need to confess and seek forgiveness from the other marriage partner, and *anyone* else you have involved or hurt, such as parents or children old enough to understand the situation. Your forgiveness from your marriage partner, if it hopefully ever comes, will likely come only after you have demonstrated over a long period of time, that you have put your adultery behind you *and have not done it or anything like it again.* Hopefully, the offended spouse will have enough forgiveness and understanding in his or her heart to help ease the pain and make the burden lighter. In so doing, the marriage is likely to be saved, and can become strong again.

In counseling situations I have seen strong marriages survive adultery, but it is not easy. In fact, it is really tough. Many marriages will not survive the ordeal. And you can bet that Satan will be there to make it even more difficult. It takes a loving and forgiving marriage partner as well as a genuine willingness to truly change on the part of the wrongdoer. Some marriages have even been made stronger after adultery, if you can imagine that! Through the repentance process, marriage partners quite often finally learn how to communicate with each other for the first time. They can also finally learn how to better serve each other.

On the other hand, why can't those who marry either learn before marriage, or soon thereafter, to really communicate with and really serve each other? (We evidently once knew how to do both before our life on earth, because if we didn't, we would have joined Satan and his forces and never had the opportunity to come to earth to experience mortality). A course in Basic Communication 101 should be required before any marriage license is issued! Marriage is the most important relationship any two members of the opposite sex can enter into, and yet it is the one relationship that people are most woefully prepared to enter. I find that interesting, don't you?

There are many scriptures which indicate that marriage between a man and a woman is ordained of God (see Genesis 1:27-28; 2:23-24; Malachi 2:14-16; Matthew 19:4-6; Romans 7:1-4 and others). There are no scriptures that suggest or even hint that same sex marriages are ordained of God. *Anyone presently involved in sexual relationships outside an ordained marriage between a man and a woman, including heterosexual and/or homosexual relationships, are in danger of the Judgement* (again, see 1st Leviticus 18:22-24 and again 1st Corinthians 6:9-10). If you are in one of those relationships, *get out of it as soon as possible*, for you are involved in serious sins that will eternally destroy you!

Again, if adultery is your problem, do not hesitate to seek professional help. Select your professional help carefully through prayer and asking questions of religious leaders, trusted friends or experienced older people. Be sure that both partners are in agreement as to the type of counseling to be given and as to the type of quality possessed by the person or persons giving the counseling. By all means, do not select some highly biased counselor or therapist. Try to find someone who is more of a real spiritual type of person (not a "spiritualist") and one who is well-grounded in the doctrine of Christ, and experienced in marriage counseling. The healing process which you must go through will not only require real and honest behavioral change, but will require a positive spiritual change as well.

Remember the adulterous woman whom the Savior forgave in John Chapter 8:1-11? Among other lessons to be learned in these scriptures, two important points pertain to our present topic. The first, albeit a long one, is that when the accusers left the scene, Jesus asked her where her accusers were and had any condemned her? Her response was, "No man Lord." All the accusers left because they all evidently had sins from which they each had not repented from, and thus no one could throw any stones, let alone the first stone. But through the power of the Holy Ghost the woman recognized Jesus Christ as the Lord, the one person having the power and authority to offer her complete forgiveness. In so doing and with a properly repented heart, she was forgiven. Jesus Christ frankly forgave her because He knew of her sincerity and the depth of her faith and repentance.

The lady's repentance and forgiveness came unusually quick, for the scriptures indicate she was caught in the act. However, as indicated earlier, today true forgiveness from adultery usually comes only after demonstrating fidelity over a long period of time. We must remember that the lady received her forgiveness from the Savior himself. He gave her His undivided attention. And only He could look into her heart and determine her faith and depth of her repentance. He could do the same for you and me, if He were still on the earth, but He is not. We must therefore, work with those who truly represent the Lord on this earth, *as well as sincerely pray to God in the name of Jesus Christ,* that we might eventually receive His forgiveness. His forgiveness is necessary for us to become truly clean and for us to then be able to go forward making our life more productive, and also before we are eventually presented to the Father by Jesus Christ.

Today, by the Spirit, we can also receive forgiveness from God and/or Jesus Christ for many of our sins, and it is through our own personal revelation. When we receive Their forgiveness we will feel clean and at peace within ourselves. *That is the feeling that you will receive when you have been truly forgiven.* You do not necessarily have to be verbally told by the Lord or even God Himself that you are forgiven. *But remember, in order for you to permanently receive the forgiveness, you must strive very hard to never do the same sin again. You can not return to the same sins without receiving more condemnation and eventual punishment for the repeated offenses.*

The second lesson from the Lord's account in John is that the woman was told after not being condemned by the Savior, "go and sin no more." To emphasize the last statement in the above paragraph, to truly repent, we cannot return to the same sins, otherwise it is as if we had not repented and we must then suffer for the original and all the subsequent sins. We thus have sins heaped upon sins.

I hope that the lady of attention in the account by John, sincerely changed her behavior and then lived the rest of her life as a righteous lady. In my heart, I believe she did.

As a final point before leaving the 7th Commandment, adultery usually starts out with sexy, nasty and even filthy thoughts. Satan has a wonderful way of getting those inappropriate thoughts into our mind on an every-day basis. He is especially good at casting those thoughts into our mind with the hopes that he can get us to act on them. He wants to bring us down to his level, which is the lowest of all levels. *This is the level where inexpressable sadness and sorrow await everyone who goes there, from which you might never return! Don't you go for his bait,* for sexy, nasty and filthy thoughts are his bait. They are intended to hook you and eventually lead you carefully down to his miserable level. And endless misery is what "Hell" really is. He is just fishing for us. Stay away from his bait at all costs.

You may not always be able to control the thoughts that come into your mind, but you can control how long those thoughts stay and what those thoughts can cause you to do. On the other hand, if you persist in watching pornographic material, in *any* form, you are setting yourself up to have all kinds of filthy and nasty thoughts which can lead to your being shackled by the chains of Satan, to become as miserable as he is. Remember, remember, oh remember, that Satan has many filth pervayors in today's world seeking not only your money, but your mind, body and spirit. Many of those people work in Hollywood, and their increasing filth is slickly delivered to you in magazines, videos, DVDs, CDs, movies, broadcast T.V. and the internet. Stay away from it because it is enticing and yet every bit as dangerous as a poisonous serpent. Discipline your resolve to avoid all, even slightly pornographic materials. Actively fight against it. If we don't, it will soon take over our lives and the lives of our children.

If through self discipline you gain in strength over your thoughts, you will have fewer inappropriate thoughts to deal with.

We can be condemned by our thoughts only to the extent that we act unrighteously on them. Righteous people can control the thoughts that enter into their mind by singing or humming a song, by reciting poetry, by talking out loud, by focusing their mind on righteous things, by actively doing something constructive, by doing something that will take their mind off their sexy, nasty or even filthy thoughts. The real difference between a righteous man or woman and a filthy or unrighteous man or woman is how well he or she controls their thoughts. *And righteous people are almost always more happy than filthy or unrighteous people.* You can happily depend upon it!

The next time you get inappropriate thoughts, and you will get them, you will know who gave them to you. Then think carefully what they are encouraging you to do. Think carefully about your thoughts. When they suggest that there is no harm in acting out your sexy, nasty or filthy thoughts, know for sure that Satan is behind it. Remember, that the way to Hell starts out, oh so innocently. *You have been given the light of Christ to know good from evil, as has every person who has ever lived (see John 1:9, 3:18-21, 8:12).* Work hard on controlling your thoughts. Again, he or she who controls their own thoughts controls themselves. Seek for greater control over your thoughts through dedicated prayer and fasting. It can be done over time. *If you gain this self-control, it will be one of the greatest accomplishments you can make and one of the greatest blessings you can have.*

8th Commandment

"Thou shalt not steal." Exodus 20:15

Phil loved the new Parts Mart store that had just recently been built near his home. Almost everything he ever wanted was available in that store. In fact, when he was off work, Phil often enjoyed just strolling down the spacious isles in the store while looking at all the wonderful "stuff."

Sure enough, as time went on, Phil began to notice that the store personnel seldom walked down certain isles. And these were the isles that contained some of the most prized tools and gadgets in the entire store. The more Phil visited these isles, the more Phil wanted the "stuff." Now, Phil was not a rich man. His small income was gone by the end of each month. In fact, Phil had to budget his spending very carefully.

One day Phil just had to have some of those wonderful tools and gadgets. As he entered the store on a rainy day with a big umbrella and trench coat, he went directly to his favorite isles. He filled his pockets and the umbrella with the most expensive items. No one even seemed to notice Phil, yet he was familiar with many of the store personnel. Phil was able to walk out of the store with a few hundred dollars worth of merchandise.

When Phil finally got to his car his heart was rapidly beating with all the excitement. He had gotten away with it. No one suspected him, especially Phil, to have stolen so much "stuff."

However, a few days later Phil started to feel badly about what he had done. Just to look at any of the items he had stolen caused Phil to feel very uncomfortable. He began to recall that when he was just a kid, his dad caught him after stealing candy from the local Five-and-Dime store. His dad had made him take all the candy he had back to the store. His dad even made him confess and apologize to the store manager. Further, as a consequence for eating some of the candy, which could not be replaced, Phil had to go down to the store every day for a month to sweep the floors.

Phil could still remember how badly he felt when he was still a kid. He had shamed himself in front of his dad, the store manager and God. However, Phil also remembered how good he had felt when the a month of cleaning and sweeping floors was over. The manager even gave him some gum for working so hard, for not missing any days and especially for being so sorry and confessing that he had stolen the candy.

Now, Phil felt terrible, even with all his gadgets. He felt so bad that he wanted to have those wonderful repentant feelings again, as he had when he was a youth. He wanted them now, immediately, for what he had done at the Parts Mart store. The very next day Phil called the store manager and asked to meet with him. Phil had made the decision to talk with the manager and get his forgiveness rather than just secretly replace all the "stuff" he had stolen. Phil returned all the tools and gadgets when he met with the manager. Phil even started to cry, saying to the manager that he was ready to go to jail if necessary. The store manager was so taken back with all this confession. He was a bit angry at first at Phil for his stealing. But the manager was also thankful and humbled that this man would go to such length to repent of what he had done. In fact, after Phil had wiped the tears from his eyes, the manager offered Phil a good paying job to take care of the isles that seemed to have no employees. Phil was so confused, and yet so happy, for he was expecting to go to jail for what he had stolen, and in reality, he should have gone to jail. Stealing in any form is against man's laws and also against God's laws. But mercy is a wonderful thing and it has been known to change people for the good. Phil is very lucky that the manager had a lot of mercy.

Phil is now the most respected employee in the store. It is a good thing that the manager *never did tell anyone* about the incident, which to Phil, was also a wonderful thing. No one in the store knew the full story about Phil. All the other store employees just knew him as the best employee and most trusted person in the store.

The above case study illustrates today how easy it is to steal. Many people do it, not only for the gain it gives them in material things, but also for the thrill it gives them when they don't get caught. Unfortunately, stealing impacts all others who shop at the places where people steal, through higher prices to compensate for the stolen merchandise. No matter how one justifies or rationalizes taking things that do not belong to one's self, stealing is wrong and those who steal in this life and get away with it, will "pay for it" in the next life. All those who presently steal and get away with it will someday surely stand before the Judgement Bar of God with great fear and sorrow. If you have stolen in the past, *return or at least replace the value of what you have stolen, and then don't steal again, ever again!*

When was the last time you took something, or borrowed something from someone and then never did return it? Is that considered stealing? Have you broken one of the Twelve Commandments? In the very strictest sense, you have stolen, thus you have technically broken the Eighth Commandment. On the other hand, Webster's New World Dictionary, 1996 edition, defines stealing as:

"1. To take or appropriate (another's property, ideas, etc.) without permission, dishonestly, or unlawfully, esp. in a secret or surreptitious manner; 2. To get, take, or give slyly, surreptitiously, or without permission; 3. To take or gain insidiously or artfully."

According to Webster, stealing is thus, the taking of something "without permission," or the obtaining of something "surreptitiously," or secretly. If you borrowed something without permission, then that is technically stealing and you have broken the Eighth Commandment.

What if you borrowed something with permission, but still did not return the item. Is that technically stealing? Well, maybe not according to Webster, but have you still done wrong in not returning the borrowed item? Yes, you have! And in order to repent of it, you will need to return the item or pay for what it would cost to replace it. If you don't, maybe you are technically guilty of stealing, and will eventually be held accountable for it.

What if you took something without permission, but then later returned it, is that stealing? Technically, yes, it is stealing. But the fact that you returned the item might possibly mitigate the severity of the sin. This is especially so if the item is returned immediately and confession is made upon returning the item, as in the case study above. Well then, does it matter as to how long it was between the time you stole the item and when you returned or paid for it? Interesting question for which I am not 100% sure what the correct answer is, although I basically believe it does matter.

The more immediate that which was stolen is returned or paid for, the better. What do you think?

While I was in graduate school and during my first couple of years of teaching at the university level, I became aware that certain professors would often "steal" ideas from graduate students and even from other professors and then publish those ideas for their own credit. Stealing ideas from others is just as bad as stealing property from them. There are many professors who need to repent, although I am sure they would disagree. They would likely ask me, "Do you really consider this stealing?" "But of course." I would say.

On 10 November of 1990, concerning Martin Luther King Jr, the New York Times printed an article indicating that "substantial parts of Dr. King's Dissertation and other academic papers from his student years appear to have been plagiarized." Mr King's Ph.D. degree was later rescinded. So, even great leaders can fall prey to the sin of stealing, even though some uniformed people still believe plagiarism is not "that bad," it is still stealing.

In any case, it is sinful to steal. But these are the kinds of questions the Eighth Commandment can cause one to ask and try to answer. These types of hair-splitting arguments and commandment gradations can cause problems today as they did for the Jewish elders of long ago. This very situation of hair-splitting and commandment gradations most likely caused the Jewish elders to add even more rules, laws and directions. This had a tendency to further blind the Jews from living according to the spirit of the law and concentrate only on the letter of the law. Jesus Christ even taught this concept in the New Testament, as mentioned earlier in the book. I feel that most people of today do not even think about whether or not there are different gradations of stealing. I further feel that most people will unfortunately steal when given an opportunity, as long as they are sure they will not get caught.

Many of today's youth steal without any conscience. They have not been taught that stealing is not only against the law, it is a gross sin in the sight of their Creator. Parents of today, in general, have done a very poor job of teaching their youth the importance and the reasons for not stealing (see Romans 2:20-21). It is unfortunate that most of the parents of these youth do not know themselves the reasons for not stealing, other than to not get caught! *What a shame, for we have all been commanded by our God to not steal.* That should be reason enough not to steal, but it evidently is not enough (see Ephesians 4:28).

I feel that serious stealing, or premeditated or planned stealing is a more serious condition than is, let's say "spur-of-the-moment stealing." However, the intent of the person doing the so called "stealing" is usually not addressed in cases of theft, such as in the case of murder. I have always thought this anomaly to be interesting. I further feel that this is why the statements "without permission" or "surreptitious" have had to be stressed in today's definition of stealing. They universally cover all forms of stealing, premeditated or "spur-of-the-moment."

There are two interesting verses in Proverbs 6:30-31 that indicate that a thief should not be despised by man if he steals to "satisfy his soul when he is hungry." But, if the stealer is found, it is written, that he or she is to repay sevenfold of that which was stolen, and even "give all the substance of his house." Wow! There is no additional insight given in the scripture as to whether the man was hungry in his soul for gospel teachings, or whether he was just hungry for food. In either case, it is thus interesting to know that such a person in the Old Testament was not to be despised by man for stealing, but would be forced to repay so much back.

There have been many in the past who have stolen in order to eat and some have been caught and prosecuted to the fullest extent of the law. This seems unfair, especially when compared today to those in business who steal and swindle millions of dollars away from unsuspecting investors or share holders only to have their hands slapped or to have them spend a short time in jail, if they are caught. It seems to me that the severity of the punishment for stealing should be calculated according to the reason for the stealing and for the amount of suffering experienced by those who have suffered from the stealing. However, the reader should remember that stealing in any form, is a serious sin. If it was not, stealing would not have been one of the original Ten Commandments. In any case, I am content in the belief that God will eventually judge the intent of our heart when it comes to sins such as stealing. If greed and selfishness are the root of our stealing, and generally I believe they are, then I feel that our punishment will be greater than if our stealing is to in some way help another person, or to feed one's self or to feed family members.

Recently there have been three different national incidents in which people, who have found bags full of money and checks, returned them to their rightful owners, the owners being a bank and two large brokerage houses. In two of the cases, the money and checks amounted to over one million dollars. The "thanks" the two honest people received was little more than a verbal "thank you." In the other case, and only after pressure from the press, the person was given $100.00 for his honesty. The point here is that two of the honest people did not expect to be paid for their honesty. They did it because "It was the honest thing to do." Hooray for them, and don't you call them dumb like I heard many people call them, for they are *Commandment Keepers* and it will be well for them at the time of judgement! The third person evidently had a bit greater temptation working on him before he was able to return the money. But at least, in all three cases, the money was returned, and it was done within a short period of time.

Nationally syndicated writers jumped on the incidents and pompously castigated the public's prevailing feeling that large rewards should have been given to the three "honest" people. It is easy to be pompous when you have a steady job and money in the bank, which however, was not the case for the three "honest" people. Thus, the test of their honesty was even greater than what often is the case. Over one million dollars is a lot of money. However, the three people did receive their satisfying intrinsic reward of knowing they did the "right" thing in returning that which was not rightfully theirs to keep. Also, all three of the "returnees" likely slept well the night they turned over the money to the authorities.

Probably the most interesting fact to come out of each incident was the totally indifferent attitude that the bank and the two brokerage houses had toward each returnee. Whether a large reward was given or not given, or even expected on the part of the returnees, these are not the real issues of concern.

The real issue to the author is that if there had been a "big deal" made about the incidents by the bank and the brokerage houses, honesty could have been greatly lauded. Everyday examples of goodness and honesty should be lauded and extolled by the press and T.V. so that people, especially our young people, will know *that it is still okay to be honest.* Make sure that you are *always* honest and become one who can *always* be depended upon.

There are rewards in life that are equal to and even greater than money, and the bank and brokerage houses could have easily given them. However, these institutions failed to realize this and thus, failed to take the opportunity to extol the virtue of honesty among all three "returnees." The general public could have greatly benefitted from what the bank and brokerage houses could and should have done. It is a shame that so little was done to reward honesty, especially when the rewards were sincerely not expected on the part of the "returnees" and could have been relatively inexpensive in comparison to what was returned.

Returning to our original thinking on stealing, in one important way, stealing can be somewhat similar to murder. This is because there actually are various gradations as to the amount of premeditation that can occur prior to committing the sin of stealing. In the Old Testament, Deuteronomy 24:7, it is stated that anyone stealing a "brethren" and selling him as merchandise (kidnapping), shall be put to death. Thank goodness that even today, premeditated kidnapping is treated seriously in that it is often a lifetime sentence for those who are caught, and they are usually caught! But in most instances, as alluded to earlier, there is no legal gradation for stealing as there is for murder. I feel this is because the sin and crime of murder is so heinous that it requires gradations in order to determine the true intent on the part of the murderer.

On the other hand, in the New Testament, John 10:10, "The thief cometh not, but to steal and to kill, and to destroy. . ." Stealing is so often associated with killing, that sometimes it is hard to separate the two. Those who are caught stealing, such as bank robbers, house thieves or burglars quite often kill in order to make their get-a-way. However, stealing by itself in today's society is not considered to be as serious as murder, thus as stated above, there is no stress on the levels of premeditation for stealing.

What about the stealing of something which is not very tangible, such as a woman's virtue? Those who steal a woman's, or even a man's virtue, such as in the case of convicted rape, today are usually sentenced to life in prison. Society has little tolerance for rapists. Even incarcerated prisoners put rapists in a similar category to child molesters, who are at the bottom of the pecking order in almost all prison systems. There is no place in even uncivilized societies for rapists. They are stealers of the worst kind. A woman's or man's virtue can not be returned once it has been taken or stolen. This is likely the main reason, coupled with the fact that it is such a personal invasion, that this crime is thought to be so despicable, and is so serious before God.

Another even more intangible thing that is often stolen is time. Is the stealing of time really a serious issue? Well, in the area of business, it is calculated that there are billions of dollars lost annually because of wasted time. The waste of time in business has been calculated to be actually of greater cost than all the pilferage and loss by theft. The loss of time is the time that should have been spent on business matters that employees have spent on themselves or spent on other non-business activities, such as pornography and other things over the internet. The loss of time is also the time spent on extended coffee breaks or counterproductive discussions on personal things. Are these people breaking the Eighth Commandment? I believe they are. They take time away from the business "without permission" from the boss. It may or may not always be done in an intentional "surreptitious" or in a "secret" manner, but it is most likely done in a manner that is secret to the boss. Otherwise, it would not have been done.

What about taking paper, pencils, staplers, and pens home from work and giving them to your family members or friends? Is that stealing? "Yes," it is. Your boss would most likely be upset or fire you if he or she knew that you were taking home school or office supplies from the office to your family and/or friends. And if your boss knows what you are doing but does nothing about it, then he or she is also as guilty of breaking the Eighth Commandment as you are. Both seeing and knowing that others are stealing and then doing nothing about it, makes that person or persons accomplices to the act. Also, in so doing, these people lower their own resistance to selfishly stealing for one's self.

What about cheating on your taxes? Is that actually stealing? What about cheating the insurance company with an falsely inflated claim or cheating the phone company when you receive your quarter back when you make a call on a public phone? *Stealing in any form, whether it is for big dollars or for little quarters, is still stealing.* When you steal, you have broken the Eighth Commandment and thus need to repent of the deed. If you do not, then you as the stealer will eventually suffer the consequences, and don't kid yourself into thinking the consequences will be light.

I vividly remember the time a few years ago when I lived in Phoenix and was in a grocery line waiting to pay for some items. The lady in front of me had her purse tucked up on the back of her right arm. She was writing out a check. Her purse was open and there was a twenty dollar bill poking up out saying to me, "Hey Bill, come on, grab me. No one will see you. I'm yours to take and spend." I started to laugh because of how brazen this twenty dollar bill seemed to be or actually how brazen that nasty ole Satan was. I thus tapped the lady on the shoulder and told her she was going to lose $20.00 if she did not do something about it poking out of her purse. Of course, she thanked me and then continued to write out her check, only after which she tucked the $20.00 back into her purse.

I have since mentally reviewed that event more than once because of how brazen it was. I am sure that people of all walks of life have those kinds of temptations "thrown" at them. I believe these tests are often put in our way to measure the extent of our honesty and integrity. *When we are consistent in passing these tests, especially when honesty is concerned, the number of similar tests given to you will usually decrease.* Satan will then try other means, schemes and tests to try to get you and everyone else to break other commandments. One has to always be on his or her guard to be honest in even the small things. When we can individually evidence fidelity in small things while on this earth, we are also evidencing to God that we have the capability to eventually evidence and exercise fidelity in larger matters beyond this life.

It is interesting to read the daily newspaper in most large cities of embezzlement cases where large sums of money have been siphoned off to other "personal accounts." Now, even small cities and rural areas disclose increasing cases of the "misuse of funds." How many of these people thought they could avoid detection from simple annual audits, is beyond me. To be involved in such dishonest and selfish practices is not only stupid, it is sinful as well.

If you have a particular problem with stealing, whether it be little things or big things, remember that you will likely get caught if you continue. When you get caught, you then will be embarrassed, possibly lose your job or even go to jail. If you are "lucky" and don't get "caught," *you still know in your heart that you are a thief and just as importantly, so does God.*

If you have this problem, you need to stop stealing today! You may even need some counseling. Call a counselor today to schedule a counseling session or more. The counseling could possibly save your life.

In addition, what can you do on your own to stop this destructive behavior? The strong impulse to steal is sometimes not motivated by need or desire, it is an abnormal impulse that cannot be easily controlled. Refer back to the latter part of the chapter on the Sixth Commandment. There are three techniques discussed which may be of help to you in controlling the urge to steal. However, if you cannot control your impulses, then you need to realize that *you do* need help through professional counseling. Get it *now*. Do not delay!

If you are a parent and you have a son or daughter who steals, then make him or her face the consequences of his or her stealing today, before he or she becomes an adult and starts stealing big-time. *There are many parents today, who if they would only teach and require their children to confess to those they have stolen from and return all they have stolen, or work off the equivalent of what they have stolen, would dramatically increase honesty in the world.* These parents would also increase their own happiness in their later years in knowing they have honest children and in not having to watch them go to prison for stealing.

If you steal in order to feed some terrible habit, like drinking, drugs or sex, you especially need help now! If this is your condition, then by all means before it is too late, get some professional help. Seek help from a therapist or counselor who specializes in kleptomania, or drug, or alcohol, or sex problems. Check first with state agencies or with church counseling services. If you are unsuccessful, look in the Yellow Pages. Whatever you do, *do it today, before it is too late to do anything constructive.*

9th Commandment

"Thou shalt not bear false witness against thy neighbor." Exodus 20:16

Kirston wanted to be on the cheer team at her high school in the worst way. But Kirston couldn't dance as well as the other girls and she also was on the chubby side. However, this did not deter Kirston in any way. She thought her chances were just as good as anyone else's.

One afternoon when Kirston was thinking of a strategy to help increase her chances to be selected, she started telling lies about the other girls. She spread rumors that two of the girls had been doing some nasty things with some of the football players. She told one of the teachers who would judge the selection of the girls that three of the girls had secret drug problems. She also told the principal that two of the girls often cheated on their tests in their chemistry class and that one of the girls was pregnant and was seeking an abortion.

When the day for the tryouts finally came, Kirston thought she had done a pretty good job on the other girls. She thus thought she had a pretty good chance to make the team.

As all the girls and judges seated themselves in readiness for the tryouts, the principal stepped up to the mike to make an announcement. His announcement stunned everybody, especially Kirston. The principal stated that since most of the girls who were trying out for the team had some serious problems, the team tryouts would be canceled. There would not be a cheer team for the current year. Wow!

Kirston felt badly. Her terrible lies had caused everyone to suffer, as lies usually do. She couldn't sleep at night. Her feelings of shame and guilt were eating her alive. Every minute she thought about what she had done. The next day she decided to do something about it, even if it might cost her dearly.

Kirston made an appointment with the principal and arrived 10 minutes early. When the principal finally showed up, he took Kirston into his office. Kirston began to cry as she told the principal what she had done. She asked for his forgiveness. The principal said he could not give forgiveness and that, even if he could, it would not be right. He explained that the forgiveness for what she had done would have to come from the girls about whom she had lied.

For the next week, Kirston went to each girl and told what she had said about her. Kirston explained that she did it because she wanted very much to be on the cheer team. She further explained that she was very sorry for what she had said and asked each girl for her forgiveness. Some of the girls frankly forgave her, but most did not. Those who did not give their forgiveness started telling their own lies about Kirston. Kirston soon personally found how hurtful lies could be. She also lost what few friends she had.

After all was said and done, Kirston asked herself if she had done right by going to the principal and to the girls themselves to apologize. She knew she had been wrong in her lying about people, regardless of the reason, but she wondered about going to the principal and girls. Kirston finally concluded that she did the right thing by telling the principal and the girls about the lies she had told. Furthermore, Kirston went back to the principal and again told him that she was sorry, and that she had learned a very powerful lesson. She also wrote a letter to each girl to again apologize. However, this time she did not ask for their forgiveness.

Kirston felt a lot better about herself. She could even sleep at night. She also promised herself that she would *never* again tell lies about anyone. And, she never did tell another lie.

The particular case study above is only one of a thousand ways to illustrate how people tell lies, either to convince themselves about something or to put someone else in bad favor. Lying is so common today that many people do not honestly know the difference between truth and lies. If you, the reader, consciously tell lies, even if they are only little "white lies," then continue reading.

To bear false witness is to lie, or to not tell the truth. To "bear false witness against thy neighbor" is to lie to, or lie about your neighbor, friends, family, or anyone. The scriptures are quite plain about what the Lord Jesus Christ, or Jehovah, feels about liars. In Proverbs 6:16-19, it says:

"These six things doth the Lord hate: yea, seven are an abomination to him: A proud look, a lying tongue, and hands that shed innocent blood, An heart that deviseth wicked imaginations, feet that be swift in running to mischief, A false witness that speaketh lies, and he that soweth discord among brethren."

It is interesting to note that of the seven things that are abominable to the Lord, lying is mentioned twice, plus "he that soweth discord among brethren" is usually a liar or gossiper. Thus, to lie or gossip is to do that which the Lord hates.

One can generally lie in two ways. The first is the usual way in which one tells untruths about things, events or about people. Whether the "untruths" or lies are said intentionally or even unintentionally, the end result of lying is still the same. The end result in it's least form, is not good for someone. Someone is almost always injured by lies. A typical work office in a large company, or even in a small company, a school or school district, a college or university are all fertile grounds for telling lies about people. *People often tell lies to make themselves look good in the eyes of others, or to seemingly protect themselves, or to intentionally injure others.* Sadly, there are many politicians in this country and in all countries of the world who have lied under all three of the situations mentioned above and as defined in Proverbs. Many of them have become master lairs, with the best and biggest lies often going to the largest body of constituents. Even some of our most recent Presidents have been strongly accused and even prosecuted for lying under oath in order to protect themselves from their gross immoral behaviors, or to in some way protect the Office of the President.

On the other hand, our President Barack Hussein Obama has been a consistent liar, especially when he said several times to the American public that "You can keep your present medical plan, you can even keep your own Doctor." Of course, this was a big fat lie among many others he has told, thus continuing the diminishment of the Office of the Presidential.

Lying seems to be on the rampant increase in this country possibly caused by the increasing bad example of some of our leaders and the complexities in our troubled society. But nonetheless, the 9th Commandment to not lie, remains the same!

A short while back it was interesting to observe the ongoing problems with Iraq and the inspection teams looking for weapons of mass destruction. Both American and Iraqi diplomats have called each other blatant liars. And it just might depend on whether you favor the Americans or the Iraqis as to whom you think is telling the biggest or the most lies. Also, think of all the lies the tobacco industry has been telling for years to the American public and the world as well, that smoking is not bad for human beings. Think of all the lies the government has told the American public about agent orange chemicals that were used in the

Vietnam war, or all the radioactive fallout received by the "down winders" from the atom bomb blasts of the 1950s and 1960s. Think of all the lies the communist and repressive governments of Russia and China have told their citizens over the years. Lying unfortunately seems to be a way of life for not only many people on an individual basis, but for governments and whole countries as well.

I recently worked for a small college, in of all places, Colorado City, Arizona. Yes, this is the place where polygamy is practiced. While there I found it interesting to observe that in order to receive government aid for schooling, food stamps, etc., that the plural wives which followed the first wife, had to lie on their government forms as to their marital situation. I feel this situation has unfortunately generalized such that those who practice polygamy, it is okay to lie and misrepresent the truth whenever necessary. This is sad because they can and have, easily justified the sin of lying so that many polygamists don't even think twice about lying, whenever the opportunity arises.

The second way of lying is where one knowingly hears gossip or lies being said, but does nothing to stop the gossip or lies, or even willingly continues to perpetuate the gossip or lies. These are those people "that soweth discord among brethren." They are just as guilty as those who intentionally or even unintentionally start telling the "untruths" or lies in the first place. People who gossip, or continue or pass on the gossip once told to them, are in fact, liars. Governments are also guilty of this type of lying, where they purposely "sow discord among" other countries. There are many governments today who have special departments filled with people who are specifically trained in the dissemination of "misinformation." This allows a government to systematically carry out discord among other countries, or even within their own country. The country once known as Yugoslavia comes to mind. Recall where the Yugoslav people and even the whole world were lied to by the government concerning the terrible "ethic cleansing" which took place in Kosovo.

The notion of unintentionally telling lies is so common among people of today, especially among women. It is done typically in conversation through gossip, where the "gossiper" either starts or passes on information which is usually inaccurate and harmful to others. Women generally seem to have more problems with intentional gossip which is specifically intended to hurt or injure someone. *Gossip in any form is extremely destructive, and people are consistently injured by it! People are never helped through gossip, even if the gossip is true!* A general rule I try very hard to live by is that *if I do not have anything good to say about a person, then it is best left unsaid.* You are strongly encouraged to adopt the same or a similar philosophy because it has been a real blessing to me and it will be to you also.

If you like to gossip, then you should stop today before you hurt someone. There are many people who have been very unfairly injured by gossip. If you have personally been injured from gossip, then you know what it is like to be injured. However, if you have been a party to someone else's injury, due to your gossip, then you need to repent. *You need to go to that person and apologize, and then seek his or her forgiveness.* Do it today, *then don't ever gossip again.*

I have always liked opinionated people, even though I often disagree with their opinions. I like them because I at least know "where they are coming from." Whereas, one who participates in gossip, usually does not have an opinion, but he or she often puts his or her own spin on the gossip information as they pass it on to others, who do likewise. And, of course, the end result is that someone is usually hurt by it.

If you presently gossip, again, cease today. *Even if you think you don't gossip, but like to talk a lot about other people and their problems, cease doing it today!* Repent and ask for forgiveness from those you have possibly injured or damaged through your gossip. Also, ask for forgiveness from your Heavenly Father. On both counts, it will take courage, but you can, and you should do it. Do it today.

The Old Testament has many references about lying or liars (see Leviticus 6:2, 19:11, Numbers 23:19, 1st Samuel 15:29, Psalms 31:18, 109:2, 119:163, etc.). In the New Testament, there are also many references pertaining to those who lie, although very few verses are found in the four Gospels. In John, however, there are two references which well address lying. In John 8:44, John wrote that when Jesus spoke to the scribes and Pharisees, He accused them of being like Satan or the devil, in that Satan was a murderer, the father of lies, and that there was no truth in him. Thus, when you lie, you are doing what Satan does, and, although he is very good at it, he is never-the-less a terrible thing to model or copy. *Remember, that the more you do what Satan does, the easier it becomes to continue what you are unfortunately doing, and thus the more you become like Satan, who is the father of all lies and liars*. Now, if you have any of the above problems of lying and gossiping, ask yourself if you really want to continue lying or gossiping? Do you really want to do what Satan wants you to do or become? I hope that you don't, and are willing to change your ways if you do.

In John 8:55, Jesus further indicates that He would be a liar like the scribes and Pharisees if He told them He did not know the Father. But Jesus continued, "...But I know him, and keep his saying." Evidently, Jesus did not like liars or those who have any part in lies.

In his writings, Paul had much to say about lying. In Acts 5:3, Paul asks Ananias "why has Satan filled thine heart to lie to the Holy Ghost...?" He then tells Ananias that "...thou has not lied unto men, but unto God." Upon hearing the words of Paul, Ananias fell down and died. I would not want to be in Ananias's shoes when the Judgement Day comes, for lying to the Holy Ghost and to God are the most serious of all sins. (Can you imagine the pain, the burning sensation, the terrible feelings, the "hell" that Ananias has felt all these years since he told his big lie?) And he still has to await that which will be given him at judgement time. Wow, that is a horrible thought to contemplate. This is especially horrible for Ananias, for in Matthew one learns that there is no forgiveness in this life or in the life to come for lying to, denying or blasphemy against the Holy Ghost (see Matthew 12:31-32, Mark 3:29, and Luke 12:10).

In Titus 1:2 we are told by Paul that God cannot lie. What a wonderful thing to know, that everything that God our Eternal Father, His son Jesus Christ or the Holy Ghost say, is truth. All three of them are holy vessels of truth wherein They cannot lie. Wouldn't this world be a wonderful place if everyone always told the truth? Think how much nicer your job environment or your school would be if all your work colleagues or college classmates and professors told the truth all the time. Wouldn't your family also benefit if everyone in the family told the truth all the time? It would be fantastic! We can all learn to live with "nothing but the truth." But then, what about you? Do you tell the truth all the time? You should, even if the truth hurts. One can still use a great deal of tact and sensitivity when it is necessary to tell truths that hurt. Try it the next time you are tempted to lie or to even knowingly be a part of lie. *Tell the truth always and remember, that if it is not necessary to tell a truth that will hurt, then do not tell it!*

In 1st John 2:21-22, we understand that to deny that Jesus is the Christ, is to lie. One who also denies the Father and the Son is an Antichrist. Wow! How would it be to be called an Antichrist at Judgement Day? Those who deny the Father and His son Jesus Christ are liars. *Don't you ever be that kind of a liar!* If you do, you will regret it for maybe the rest of eternity.

In Revelations 21:7-8, we learn that liars along with murderers, whoremongers (those who have intercourse with whores or prostitutes), idolaters (those who worship idols or have an excessive devotion to or reverence for some person or thing), "shall have their part in the lake which burneth with fire and brimstone: which is the second death." These folks will not live eternally with Father nor with His son Jesus Christ. And someday they will eternally regret their decisions to be the kind of people they once became or have now become. But, if you are one of these people, you still have enough time to repent and change. You really can, but you have to sincerely believe it, *and then do your very best for the rest of your life,* however short or long it may be. And may you be blessed and strengthened in your efforts.

In Revelations 22:14-15, verse 14 discusses that those who live the commandments will have the right to the tree of life and may enter into the gates of the city of God our Father. In verse 15, it discusses those "...sorcerers, and whoremongers, and murders, and idolaters, and whosoever loveth and maketh a lie" are the same as dogs and will be left out of the city of God. Those who lie and those who love lies will have the same fate to dread on Judgement Day.

What about those little "white lies" that my sweet Grandmother Lewis told me about many years ago? Webster's New World

Dictionary actually states that a white lie is "a lie concerning a trivial matter, often one told to spare someone's feelings." Are "white lies" any more acceptable to God than "non-white lies?" Interesting question. Maybe they are, but I would recommend that anyone who is good at telling little "white lies" be extremely careful when they are told. I would further recommend that it would be a good thing to terminate the practice as soon as possible and never return to it. As we all know, little things usually lead to bigger things; those little "white lies" usually lead to bigger and even more serious lies. We can get easily sucked into telling bigger "non-white lies" before we know it. So, don't tell even those little "white lies" any more.

Those who tell lies almost always have to tell additional lies to cover the first lie. Lying to defend or protect one's inappropriate behavior can become a perpetual thing that usually leads to disaster. A recent former U.S. President and even the current president are good cases in point. *In any form, lying is bad and should be stopped immediately!*

People often tell lies to remove themselves from difficult or trying situations, or to protect themselves following displays of inappropriate or defective behaviors, as was mentioned earlier. These are called "defensive" lies. However, these types of lies are not much different from "offensive" lies that are told to intentionally hurt or defame someone or something, or to make one's self look better than he or she really is. Sure, there may be more viciousness behind those lies intended to hurt someone, but the fact remains that when you do not tell the truth in any form, it is a sin, and a gross sin at that. If you tell either "defensive" or "offensive" lies, you need to stop telling them this very day! *You really can find something else, which is much more positive, to do with your mouth than to tell lies.*

Children of today often do not know what real truth is because they are exposed to so much lying from their parents, athletes, adult figures, heros, industries, politicians, governments and especially T.V. "If everybody does it, what is the big thing about it?" said one young man to me about lying when I was doing research for this book. He is right, unfortunately! But, as children of God, we all have to become much more honest in all we do. Parents also need to teach their children the importance of always telling the truth, regardless of what other people or even governments do. We need to *tell the truth all the time*, again, even though it hurts us or others, when it is necessarily told. However, we all can and should be respectful and sensitive when we tell truths that hurt. Again, if a particular truth could hurt someone, if told, and if it is not necessary to repeat it, then don't repeat it. Even though you might be telling the truth, if you pass the information on as gossip, which might be harmful or hurtful to someone, then you are a gossiper. And remember, the one who gossips is the same as a liar.

We may, and probably will, personally suffer when we tell truths that hurt. There have been many who have actually lost their good positions and even their jobs because they have told the truth. Is it worth it to lose your job for telling the truth? Well, maybe in this world it may sometimes seem that it is not worth it; however, when we get to the next world, I am quite sure that it will have been worth it. In fact, you can even safely bet your mortgage on it, although I do not necessarily condone betting. But, I have actually, although indirectly, bet my mortgage when it was necessary. Not that I actually bet my mortgage, but I have told truths wherein I have lost my job because of them, and thus was not able to pay my mortgage for a while. Thus, remember the scripture in First Corinthians 2:9 which gives us reason for telling the truth, as well as reason for living all the commandments, where it says:

"But as it is written, Eye hath not seen, nor ear heard of man, the things which God hath prepared for them that love him."

Read also the 64th chapter of Isaiah in which there is a great and beautiful prayer and pleading from Isaiah for Israel, and for you and me. *Always keep your heavenly goals in mind as you are working your way through life, even with all of its challenges and pitfalls.* May God bless you in your efforts to be truthful.

10th Commandment

"Thou shalt not covet thy neighbor's house, thou shalt not covet thy neighbor's wife, nor his manservant, nor his maidservant, nor his ox, nor his ass, nor any thing that is thy neighbor's." Exodus 20:17

Whenever Gary drove his red convertible through the neighborhood, Tony would imagine himself driving it instead of rich 'ole Gary. Tony liked Gary's car better than just about anything. He really had to have it someday.

Two years had put some size and weight on Tony. He was now considered to be the "big guy" in the neighborhood. As Tony walked home from school one day with some of his friends, he saw Gary's car parked at the local bar. Evidently, Gary was inside playing pool with some of the local boys. Tony's friends said how cool it would be to drive Gary's car around for a while. Tony agreed. With a fast hot-wire job, Tony and his friends were riding around in Gary's red convertible.

When Gary left the pool hall, he quickly returned to call the police to report his missing car. As Tony and his friends approached an intersection, a police car pulled up behind them. The police officer was at that moment receiving the stolen car report. He turned on his red light and motioned for the boys to pull over. Tony panicked. He sped off with the officer in hot pursuit. Tony soon reached 80 miles an hour on the city streets. He tried his best to make the curve, but couldn't. The car hit the side of a building and all the occupants were thrown out of the car and killed.

Had Tony been able to control his desire to obtain Gary's car, he and his friends would be alive today. But Tony had a problem in coveting the nice things that belonged to other people. However, the problem became serious when Tony could not, nor did he want to control his desire to have what someone else possessed.

In almost every situation, to covet means to intensely desire something that someone else has, something that you do not have. The process of coveting is bad because it indicates a selfish heart. But coveting often leads to more serious sins that are often committed in obtaining the coveted things. Murder, adultery, stealing, lying, and even kidnapping children are unfortunately the all-too-often results of uncontrolled coveting. Those who do the above sins may not fully pay for them in this life, but for those who do not repent from these sins and change their ways, the great sadness of the eternities awaits them. Eternity is a lot longer than the time you will have on earth to repent from your sins! *If you have trouble with coveting, first plan on repenting and then start making permanent changes in your behavior today.*

The Tenth Commandment, as stated above, gives an indication of the time frame in which the commandment was first given with the references to oxen and asses. However, today, not much has really changed from the original commandment with the exception that we have many more things to covet than people had during the time of Moses. A man or woman's house, a man's wife or a woman's husband, or a man or woman's servant are situations which remain pretty much the same today as in yesteryear. On the other hand, people at the time of Moses didn't have fancy cars and trucks, flashy Nike shoes and clothes, sophisticated musical instruments, powerful computers, incredible stereo equipment, complex cameras, expensive watches, beautiful color H.D.T.V.s with DVDs, and many other wonderful things that most people want very much to own.

Today, people like to have all the above things so much so that they are often willing to steal, kill and/or lie to get them. When you add the nasty mix of prevalent addicting drugs and alcohol, the situation can truly become serious and dangerous as well. Addicted people will often do terrible things to obtain or steal highly desired items in order to sell them to support their gross habits. Families have often been ripped apart because of a family member stealing their most precious and valued things in order to obtain the money necessary for drugs and alcohol. In these cases, very often murder and, for sure, lying, are associated with the stealing.

Wanting things is not necessarily bad, for we all want things we don't have. Most of us even want things we don't need. But when wanting leads to violence and/or stealing in order to get the desired objects, then we have uncontrolled coveting, and this is very bad for everyone. You can be sure that one really is breaking the Tenth Commandment when he or she covets in uncontrolled fashion. (My mother often cautioned me to distinguish between my wants and my needs, and sometimes it was hard to make the distinction. Maybe my mother's advice would be good for you too).

Young people who have grown up in the middle and the upper-class homes of today are used to having many of the nicer things of life. Seldom do they appreciate the hard work and sacrifice that their parents have spent over long periods of time in accumulating the "nicer things" of life. *When this lack of appreciation is coupled with the instant gratification that T.V. fosters and glorifies, young people are just not content to wait for the future.* They want more than their parents had, and they want it now! In many cases, the desire for instant gratification leads them to commit serious sins. Adults whose childhood was spent in poverty seek instant gratification and the nicer things of life as well. Unfortunately, as they become older, smarter and stronger adults, they often victimize senior citizens or defenseless people. It is these victimized people who pay the terribly high price for those selfish adult-like children who gratify their own covetous nature by force. The high price includes the loss of trust, security and safety which, for most older people, are often more important than the possessions taken.

In addition to the Tenth Commandment as stated above in Exodus, there are several other scriptures in the Old Testament which support, time and time again, the importance of not coveting (see Proverbs 21:26, 28:16, Isaiah 56:11, Jeremiah 6:13 and Habakkuk 2:9). In the second chapter of Micah, the destruction of Israel is lamented because of the wickedness of the people. In the second verse of Chapter two, it states,

"And they covet fields, and take them by violence; and houses and take them away: so they oppress a man and his house, even a man and his heritage."

Uncontrolled covetousness by the Israelites often lead to the use of violence in order to steal that which was not theirs. They were certainly commanded to avoid it but, as often was the case, many did not heed the commandment.

In the New Testament there are some wonderful scriptures which also stress the importance of not coveting. In Luke 12:15, the Savior teaches, *"Take heed, and beware of covetousness: for a man's life consisteth not in the abundance of the things which he possesseth."* This is wonderful counsel. The measurement of a man or woman's life should not be evaluated by how many "things" of the world he or she has been able to obtain. As Jesus taught in both Matthew 16:26-27 and Mark 8:35-36, *"For what shall it profit a man, if he shall gain the whole world, and lose his own soul?"* The Savior's teaching as stated in the two scriptures above is great food for thought for all mankind to carefully consider.

In doing some basic research for this text, I interviewed several young gang members. I asked why they would ever want to become pimps and drug-pushers when they got older? I pointed out that most of these unsavory types of people don't live very long. Their unanimous answer was shocking. They *all* preferred to have a few years living "high on the hog" rather than living a long life of projected poverty and struggle. These young kids were careful observers of the big money, "babes," fancy things, and prestige their often short lived adult role models brought into their neighborhoods. The unfortunate thing is they wanted these same things regardless of the possible consequences, including that of a shortened life. Wow! That is a sad and depressing commentary on a growing segment of our society. It doesn't give one much to look forward to, especially those in the lower economic sectors of our cities.

In Romans 13:9, Paul tells as to keep the commandments. Therein he lists six of them, five of which are from the Ten Commandments, including the commandment to not covet. I am sure that Paul did not mean to tell the Romans that they could forget about living the other six commandments. It is my opinion that Paul wanted to stress these specific five commandments to those particular people of Rome at that particular time, plus add the commandment about loving your neighbor as yourself. (This is a commandment that will be addressed as the Twelfth Commandment later in the book). The emphasis that I want to make here is that Paul, the Apostle, throughout his ministry, consistently stressed living all the commandments, including the Tenth Commandment to not covet. The reader should carefully believe by now that none of the original Ten Commandments were done away by the life or death of the Savior, nor by anyone else. Jesus Christ did not do away with or remove any of the original Ten Commandments. If He had done otherwise, He would have plainly told us so in the New Testament.

Paul taught in 1st Corinthians 12:31 and 14:39, that it is acceptable to covet good things. Remember, at the beginning of this discussion of the Tenth Commandment, the definition of "to covet" was an intense desire to have what someone else has. However, it is appropriate to desire "good" things, such as greater abilities, sensitivities, skills and knowledge, especially when, once obtained through hard work and dedication, these things will be used to bless and serve others. *Therein, the key to obtain the desired attributes is to use them for the betterment of others.* It is also okay to desire "good" things if they are obtained through the usual means of prayer, study, and good old hard work. I think that the desire to do "good" is the ultimate litmus test for the commandment of covetousness. Of course, these greater abilities, skills, sensitivities and knowledge come to one only after seeking and obtaining them through dedicated effort. They do not come easily, but they are certainly worth the effort to gain them.

Do you have problems in keeping the Tenth Commandment? Do you "intensely desire" what other people have, possibly enough to take it from them? Be of good cheer, because almost everyone would like some things that their neighbors, friends, family or even strangers have. But to really covet often means that one will go to extremes to forcefully obtain those things for themselves from those who have them. Again, this is an indication of a very selfish heart and spirit. I hope the reader is not this selfish: however, if you are, and you do sometimes use force or other more sinful methods to get what you want, *then you need to repent and work to change your ways immediately*. If you have no problems with coveting, consider yourself to be blessed and be thankful for it.

11th Commandment

***"Thou shalt love the Lord thy God with all thy heart, and with all thy soul, and with all thy mind." Matthew** 22:37*

Brenda felt like she was at the end of her rope. Her husband had died just three months earlier and left her in a terrible financial mess. She did not know where to turn. To make things worse, her car had just broken down and two of her children were sick. She hated her low-paying job and there were no immediate family members from either side of the family who could help.

She wondered if life was worth living. But, she also remembered a thought she had heard long ago in some Sunday School class that "Man is that he might have joy." She thought, how can one have joy when one is faced with such big problems with seemingly no help? Feeling overwhelmed, she dropped to her knees and pleaded with God through prayer.

Brenda had always remembered to say her prayers, but this one was special. She needed help, and she needed it now, not at some time in the future. Brenda spent over one hour on her knees. When she arose, many tears had stained her blouse and her hair was a mess. But she felt that her prayer had at least gotten through the ceiling and that something positive would happen.

As she began to prepare dinner, the phone rang. Her neighbors, who were members of her church, were calling to ask if they could bring dinner over for her and the children. Before Brenda could explain that she was just starting to fix dinner, the neighbors said they would be right over. Almost before she could run a comb through her hair, the doorbell rang. Walking toward the door, she heard a still small voice whisper to her, "I have come to help you."

Her neighbors brought in bags of food which had been gathered and prepared, evidently, by many people in her church. A lot of it was put into the refrigerator for cold storage, but there were also canned goods and other foodstuffs that were put into the pantry. The neighbor husband and wife briefly sat down with Brenda to explain that two men in the church and one of their wives were going to come over the next night and help her with her financial problems. There would also be a young man who the neighbors knew who would be coming over that very night to fix her car. Also, one of the older daughters of the people across the street would stay during the school day and take care of her two sick children until they got well. This would enable Brenda to go to work. Her friends also offered to meet any additional needs if Brenda would call them and explain what she needed. They wanted to be of help and would be of help as long as she needed it and whenever she needed it.

After dinner was over and the neighbors had gone, Brenda with grateful tears in her eyes, again went to her knees. In this prayer, she thanked her Heavenly Father, in the name of Jesus Christ, for His responding to her needs and for touching the hearts of so many people to bless her family in such kind and thoughtful ways. One thing that Brenda did not know however, were the great blessings that came to each of the participants as a result of their willing and unselfish service.

In the case study above, I am quite sure that Heavenly Father must have looked down upon Brenda and appreciated her exercise in faith, her reliance on Him and her willingness to take time to express her gratitude and thanks to Him for the help she had received. As a parent, I appreciate my own children's expression of their gratitude and thanks to me for something I have done for them, and I feel that our Heavenly Father feels the same way about His children, and that includes *all of us*.

The eleventh and twelth commandments are very special. Within them are contained all the commandments. If one is faithful in diligently keeping both of them, he or she will surely be blessed, because he or she will have to be living in harmony with all the other commandments. That is the beauty of these two, higher level, great commandments as given to us by the Savior in the New Testament.

The Eleventh Commandment was given by Jesus Christ after being approached by a Pharisee who was a lawyer, who was trying to tempt Jesus. In Matthew 22:36, the lawyer asked Jesus, "Master, which is the great commandment in the law?" After stating the commandment as written on the previous page, Jesus then said, "This is the first and great commandment."

In Mark 12:28-34, the same person tempting Jesus is described as a scribe rather than a lawyer, as indicated in Matthew. However, scribes in the New Testament were often referred to as lawyers. The scriptures in Mark also show a slight deviation in what the Lord Jesus Christ said concerning the "first and great commandment." After being asked by the scribe, "Which is the first commandment of all?", Jesus answers:

"The first of all the commandments is, Hear, O Israel; The Lord our God is one Lord: And thou shalt love the Lord thy God with all

thy heart, and with all thy soul, and with all thy mind, and with all thy strength: this is the first commandment." (Mark 12:29-30.)

The version of the account in Mark indicates that Jesus specifically stated to all of Israel that "The Lord our God is one Lord," which is not stated as such in the Matthew account. (It is interesting, and certainly correct, that Jesus Christ teaches that our Father in Heaven, meaning both His literal and our spiritual Father, is one God and one Lord; not a plurality of Gods or Lords in one). (See Hebrews 1:1-5).

It should also be remembered that Jesus Christ is referred to through out the New Testament as Lord. But evidently some attempt has been made by the King James translators to try to distinguish Jesus Christ from the Father, who is referred to as LORD (small case capital letters), in the Old Testament and in some places in the New Testament (Psalms 110:1-5 and Acts 2:34-36). For instance, throughout the Old and New Testament, the title and spelling of LORD, usually referred to Jehovah. In the New Testament, the same title but different presentation of Lord, (small case small letters), usually refers to Jesus Christ. However, the two scriptures above in Psalms and in Acts, and there are others, which give indication that LORD refers to God the Father, and Lord, refers to Jesus Christ. Of course, not recognizing that Jesus Christ was the Jehovah of the Old Testament, it is understandable that the translators caused the confusion.

It should also be noted that the many words which are italicized in the scriptures, represent an attempt by the KJV translators to indicate to the reader that the translation was not perfect. That something either had to be added in English to fill out or complete a phrase or thought not existing in either Hebrew or Greek. In other cases, italics were used when English grammatical construction called for words that were not needed to make similar phrases or thoughts in Hebrew or Greek. In most instances the translators judgement was consistent with revealed truth, but in some instances it was not so.

As indicated earlier in the discussion of the Second and Third Commandments, Jesus Christ is well documented as the I AM and the Jehovah of the Old Testament. Also, it should be remembered that the Lord for Jesus Christ is none other than God the Father. He is the God and Lord of Jesus Christ. The Father is the God of all Gods and of all Lords. *However, Jesus Christ is our Lord, and it is really not accurate nor appropriate to call God, our Heavenly Father, as our Lord, although it is often done.* This explanation does not demean the Father in any way. It just is an appropriate explanation of Their correct relationship to us and to each other.

Jesus Christ is not only our Lord, He is our Savior, and our Redeemer as well. He is our advocate and intercessor with God, our Heavenly Father. There should be, and actually is nothing mysterious about Jesus Christ's relationship with and to the Father, and our relationship to both the Father and to the Son. Jesus Christ was the first born of all of Heavenly Father's spiritual children. He thus, is our eldest brother. Jesus Christ is also the literal earthly son of Heavenly Father. He is the "first born" of the Father of both His spiritual and earthly form.

Jesus noted in discussing the commandment in Mark that we should additionally love God with all our "strength." Also, this commandment in Mark is referred to as "the first commandment" and not "the first and great commandment" as in Matthew.

Of possibly more significance between the two gospel accounts, in Mark it indicates that the lawyer knew the law well and evidently repeated it back to Jesus with a positive spirit. Jesus told him in response that "Thou art not far from the kingdom of God." There is unfortunately, no additional information as to what happened to the lawyer after hearing the response from Jesus.

The same account in Luke again deviates somewhat from both the accounts in Matthew and Mark (see Luke 10:25-37). The Luke version gives no indication that Jesus stated the commandment to the lawyer as indicated in the other two accounts, only that the lawyer stated back to Jesus the commandment, and also stated that we are to love our neighbors as ourselves. In response to the lawyer's statement, Jesus answered, "Thou hast answered right: this do, and thou shalt live." But the lawyer, in the Luke account, evidently pressed Jesus further, or was "willing to justify himself," asked Jesus, "And who is my neighbor?" The response that Jesus Christ gave to him is the wonderful Parable of the Good Samaritan, which is significant because it is not found in any of the other three Gospels. Without the Parable of the Good Samaritan we would not have the wonderful examples of service and charity displayed by the Samaritan, in which we can well learn and emulate today.

The differences in the various accounts where the Two Great Commandments were given are quite interesting, but not necessarily significant from a doctrinal perspective. The only possible exception is that we are given the Parable of the Good Samaritan in the Luke account. The account of the Two Great Commandments is not mentioned as such in the book of John. However, in John 13:34-35, the following statement indicates that

John must have been fully aware of at least the spirit of the Two Great Commandments, and I'm sure he knew the "letter" of them as well!

"A new commandment I give unto you, That ye love one another; as I have loved you, that ye also love one another. By this shall all men know that ye are my disciples, if ye have love one to another."

On the other hand, all the above differences in the four gospel books well illustrate the various different interpretations the four gospel writers often had on similar events which occurred in the life of the Savior. In any case, all four Gospel writers support the fact that we are commanded by Jesus Christ to love God the Father, with all our heart, soul, mind and strength. This leaves nothing out. *In other words, we are to love God with all our capacity and ability in all that we do.*

But what does it really mean to love God? It means to live all the Twelve Commandments, it means to do as God the Father and His son Jesus Christ have said we should do in the scriptures; it means to live righteously; it means to love and treat our neighbors as we would like ourselves to be treated; it means to love and pray for those who do not like us and even persecute us; it means to help those who need help and it means to be *selfless* rather than *selfish.* It also means to control our passions and our tempers; it means to keep control of our mouth and what it says; it means to be honest and true in all our dealings; it means to be kind at all times; it means to think pure and righteous thoughts; it means to discard and shun pornography, drugs, alcohol and tobacco; it means to stop sinning and most of all, *it means to do our best to be like God and His son Jesus Christ at all times and in all places while we are on this earth.*

Well now, how are you doing with all those "it means" above? Do you feel a little uncomfortable? Well you should, in fact, we *all* should. But this does not mean that you or me, or anybody else should give up or just lay down and die because we can't do all those things all the time. *Regardless of what you have done in the past, you can still change for the good, even if your change is like a baby learning to walk by taking one small step at a time.* Even if you have done very bad things in the past, unless it is murder or sinning against the Holy Ghost, you can still fully repent and change for the good. And even if you have killed or murdered, you can stop and kill or murder no more, and you can help those who remain and those whom you have injured, and hope and pray that there might be forgiveness for you in the next world.

If you are in prison, you can still change from within yourself, even within those prison walls. You can change the inner vessel or change what is in your heart. *You can still get forgiveness from God if you apply the basic principles of repentance as outlined in the discussion of the third commandment.*

You need to pray to God, our Heavenly Father, in the name of Jesus Christ, and earnestly seek His forgiveness. It may take a long time in coming, for He often will allow you to be tested over time to see if you are really sincere in your repentance and desire to change. *God will also measure the extent of your repentance by what kind of life you live from now on.* If your heart becomes full of love and appreciation for what your Father in Heaven and His son Jesus Christ have done for you, then your life and deeds from now on will most likely reflect these great personal attributes.

Have courage. You might often be ridiculed, when you evidence in your life that you love God *first.* But remember, if you do, you will be in good company. There are many faithful men and women of God who quietly walk this earth always doing good unto others and living righteous personal lives as God would have them do. *And you can be one of them also!* It however, takes much courage, strength and persistence, *but you can do it.* You really do have the capability to live a righteous life. And Our Heavenly Father and Jesus Christ will see that you get the necessary courage and strength IF you sincerely ask for Their help through fasting and prayer, *and then put forth a lot of high quality personal effort.* May you be greatly blessed in your efforts.

12th Commandment

"And the second is like unto it, Thou shalt love thy neighbor as thyself." Matthew 22:39

Keven saw the car slide off the road and disappear down the hill. It was dark, cold and rainy and it was tempting to stay in his warm van. Yet he knew that he must help.

Keven first reported the incident over his car phone and then gathered the ropes he used in training his horses. He soon located the car, which was only half-submerged in the lake. He could hear small children crying and he knew he must act quickly.

He was able to get the three youngsters out of the back seat and onto the bank by the lake. He then concentrated on the driver and front passenger, who he assumed were the parents. But the car started to slip farther into the lake. Keven worked fast and furious and was finally able to get the father and mother safely on the bank by the lake before the car slipped under the water.

Soon after everyone was out of the car and safely onto the bank, the paramedics and ambulance finally arrived. Blankets were handed out and the family was all loaded into the ambulance. Both the father and mother were badly injured, which worried Keven. Keven followed the ambulance to the hospital where he learned the mother had died in route. He also learned that the family had no insurance. Keven took out his check book and paid for all the emergency expenses. The amount was equivalent to his house payment, which he had intended to deposit that very day.

The next day Keven contacted the County Welfare Services and United Way informing them of the unfortunate family. The staffs of both organizations assembled to organize a plan to meet the needs of the family. Keven felt good about what he had done, but still felt badly for the family. He knew there were other needs which he could not meet. However, this did not detour him from going to the local banks and radio stations to see if they would start an active fund drive for the family. They all accepted Keven's request.

It was several months later when Keven answered the knock on his door. Standing on the doorstep were three handsome youngsters and a man with a big smile. The family he had helped had all come to express their individual and collective appreciation to Keven for what he had done for them. Without his help, the family would have first died, but then following their rescue, would have had serious problems getting back on their feet. There were many tears which flowed that day and they were coupled with sincere expressions of love, appreciation and thanks.

Keven had lived the Golden Rule, "Do Unto Others, As You Would Have Them Do Unto You." He did not just think about living it, as so many of us do today, he actually lived it! And in so doing, he was truly living in full compliance with the Twelfth Commandment.

This commandment is the second of the two "Great Commandments," or the second after the "First Commandment," depending upon whether you are reading Matthew or Mark. In verse 40 of Chapter 22 in Matthew, Jesus Christ states: "On these two commandments hang all the law and the prophets." *In other words, these two Great Commandments are the most important of all the commandments.* In Mark 12:31, we read:

"And the second is like, namely this, Thou shalt love thy neighbor as thyself. There is none other commandment greater than these."

As stated earlier in the Eleventh Commandment, in John 13:34-35, we are told by Jesus Christ, as He told His disciples then, that there was a new commandment and that was to love one another as He has loved us. ***And, as He has loved us by taking upon Himself all our sins in Gethsemane and then laying down His life on Calvary, we are to, in turn, love and help others.*** Jesus Christ's love for us motivated Him to help us in so many ways. Thus, if we really want to love others, we will be found helping them. Jesus Christ has paved the way for everyone to return to The Father, that we might inherit eternal life with Them if we become worthy enough to merit this greatest of all blessings. Part of becoming worthy is that we *demonstrate love* and provide help to our families, our friends, our neighbors, yes, and even to those who make fun, persecute and ridicule us. Love and help go hand-in-hand. In Matthew 16:27, it says:

"For the Son of man shall come in the glory of his Father with his angels; and then he shall reward every man according to his works."

After the Millennium and the third Resurrection or any additional resurrections, there will be The Judgement when we all will be rewarded according to not just what we have believed on this earth, but what we have done, our works if you please (see James 2:14-26 and Revelations 2:23)! Those who are resurrected on the morning of the First Resurrection and whose works are full of charity, love, obedience, faithfulness, and genuine repentance, will likely be judged to be worthy to have eternal life with Heavenly Father and Jesus Christ. Again, this is the greatest of all blessings to mankind. Those whose resurrection is later than the morning of the First Resurrection and whose works are of lesser goodness, will live eternally, but *not* with Heavenly Father and Jesus Christ. Anyone who thinks or believes otherwise, *has not carefully studied and understood the scriptures.*

Becoming worthy of the greatest of all blessings, is not an easy thing to achieve. As was indicated earlier in this book, it takes *more* than just belief to become worthy of eternal life with God the Father and Jesus Christ. It is not only an active process, it is a proactive process, one in which we must participate every day. We *must* always do what we have been commanded to do and we *must* live *all* the commandments as best we can until our life on earth is over. In John 14:21 it says:

"He that hath my commandments, and keepeth them, he it is that loveth me: and he that loveth me shall be loved of my Father, and I will love him, and will manifest myself to him."

Since we do have the commandments, it is imperative that we must live them in order to actively express our love for our Father in Heaven and Jesus Christ. *They will love us regardless of what we do. But when we choose to be obedient and faithfully live according to Their commandments, then we have claim to all the blessings They have promised us.* In so doing, we will eventually have claim to being called worthy and inherit all that the Father has prepared for those that *evidence* that they truly love both God and His son Jesus Christ. To strive for anything less, is a waste of our earthly life and will cause one to lose out on receiving the greatest of all blessings.

A good illustration of what is discussed above can easily be made using parents who have children. It is easy to give obedient children much of what they ask for, of course, within limits. And it is easy to love them because of their obedience, but we should still love them even when they are disobedient, as the Father and Jesus Christ continue to love us when we are disobedient. On the other hand, it is difficult for us to give consistently disobedient children what they ask for when they do not appreciate much of anything, let alone merit anything because of their lack of obedience. As such, it becomes a great challenge for us as children of God to love our own disobedient children. But love them we must, even when disapproving of their behavior.

In conjunction with the Eleventh Commandment of loving God with all your heart, soul, mind and strength, and the Twelfth Commandment of loving your neighbor as yourself, these two commandments quite effectively and efficiently include all the other commandments. One who truly loves God and who truly loves his or her neighbor, will not be found killing, committing adultery, lying, stealing, coveting, dishonoring parents or the elderly, dishonoring the Sabbath day, worshiping any graven or even "ungraven" images, saying the name of God in vain or having any other gods before our Father in Heaven. *The Eleventh and Twelfth Commandments are the Two Great Commandments. They are in reality, the First Two Commandments!* It takes greater faith, greater knowledge and greater self-control to fully live them, for they encompass all the other commandments.

The Two Great Commandments are spelled out in sufficient detail for us to know the requirement of compliance and living by the spirit of the law, but not in too much detail to require only living by the letter of the law. One has to really be "in touch" with God, and with Jesus Christ, through prayer and fasting often, in order to reach the higher ground on which these two Great Commandments require us to stand.

When Jehovah gave the original Ten Commandments to Moses and the children of Israel, and vicariously to the entire family of man, the Two Great Commandments were not included. Why were they not included? It is likely that because the children of Israel had proved during Old Testament times that they could not live higher more spiritual laws, they were given more basic behavioral laws which were spelled out in very specific detail. The people in turn became more concerned with living by the letter of the law rather than by the spirit of the law. However, we in the world of today, have access to both the Old *and* the New Testaments. We are required to live not only the basic Ten Commandments; we are required to live the higher laws of the New Testament, especially the Two Great Commandments. We have been told this by the Savior himself. Thus today, we must live not only by the letter of the law, but more importantly, we must live by the spirit of the law.

On the other hand, the Jews, who did not accept Jesus Christ as the Savior or Messiah, are still living under the lower laws of carnal commandments and the incomplete Law of Moses that Jesus Christ originally gave them as Jehovah. And if you want to see detail, take an orthodox Jew aside sometime and have him explain some of the details of their commandments and laws.

Over the years since the time of Moses, various Jewish elders were responsible for adding much more detail to their commandments and laws. One can't help but admire the strict adherence that devout orthodox Jews have today in living their "specialized" commandments. However, if they only had the greater perspective and insight that the Savior Jesus Christ gave during His ministry here upon the earth. Their commandments and laws would likely be much different, a lot less complex and more straight forward, and thus more liveable today.

It is my opinion that this regal tribe of Judah of the original Twelve Tribes of Israel, the tribe that Jesus Christ Himself was born into, will someday, hopefully in the near future, realize that Jesus Christ really was Jehovah; that He is the Messiah and Savior and that He has already come to the earth to perform His first mission. Jointly, we can then all look forward to the time when He will come a second time to reclaim the earth and cleanse it from all evil and wickedness. I believe this time is on the near horizon and I further believe that many who read this book will likely experience His return. But then no one knows specifically when He will return. However, because of all the great wickedness growing even faster upon the earth today, His triumphant return has to be soon.

The beautiful but sorrowful scriptures in Matthew 23:37-39, are quite appropriate here at the end of the book and especially in light of the previous paragraph.

"O Jerusalem, Jerusalem, thou that killest the prophets, and stoned them which are sent unto thee, how often would I have gathered thy children together, even as a hen gathereth her chickens under her wings, and ye would not! Behold, your house is left desolate. For I say unto you, Ye shall not see me henceforth, till ye shall say, Blessed is he that cometh in the name of the Lord."

As a consequence of knowing the Two Great Commandments, each person hopefully will desire to become a new person, or a better person, from the inside. Living by the spirit of the law changes one internally so that he or she will want to do good always and demonstrate behaviors which are well within the letter of the law. *Just wanting to do good is not enough, we must act and do good always.* Yes, we must become a godly people. We must have God in our countenance and in all that we do. We must be "Do Gooders" in the best sense of the term. And, thank goodness for the "Do-gooders" of today, the Mother Theresas, the Albert Schweitzers, the Gordon B. Hinkleys, the Billy Grahams, the Pope, the Bob Hopes, the Anwar Sadats, the Mahatma Gandhis, the Joan Krocs, the John Huntsmans, the Hyrum Smiths and many others. The world has far too many "Wanna-bees." I think there should be a lot more "Do-Gooders," as those listed above and many more not mentioned. What does the reader think on this interesting subject? And, just who are your examples of "Do-Gooders?" How well do they match up to those people above?

Finally, what does it mean to love your neighbor as yourself in today's world? What proactive things can YOU DO TODAY to demonstrate true fidelity in living the Twelfth Commandment? Recall the parable of the good Samaritan? It is a great example of how we should live today. Jesus gave the parable in response to the lawyer who asked, "And who is my neighbor?", shortly after the lawyer had stated the Two Great Commandments. The parable is quoted from Luke 10:30-37:

"And Jesus answering said, A certain man went down from Jerusalem to Jericho, and fell among thieves, which stripped him of his raiment, and wounded him, and departed, leaving him half dead. And by chance there came down a certain priest that way: and when he saw him, he passed by on the other side. And likewise a Levite, when he was at the place, came and looked on him, and passed by on the other side. But a certain Samaritan, as he journeyed, came where he was: and when he saw him, he had compassion on him. And went to him, and bound up his wounds, pouring in oil and wine and set him on his own beast, and brought him to an inn, and took care of him. And on the morrow when he departed, he took out two pence, and gave them to the host, and said unto him, Take care of him; and whatsoever thou spendest more, when I come again, I will repay thee. Which now of these three, thinkest thou, was neighbor unto him that fell among the thieves? And he said, He that shewed mercy on him. Then said Jesus unto him, Go and do likewise."

In the example of the above parable, the good Samaritan certainly expressed love by his willingness to not only help the wounded traveler, but to take him to the inn and even pay for his expenses and promise additional payment for any other help that the traveler may have needed. Remember that the Samaritans were despised by the Jews, thus it is even more appropriate that the

Savior would choose in His parable a Samaritan to display mercy and offer help.

If any of us had been that wounded traveler, would we have wanted some merciful person to give us any less, regardless of what kind of person he or she was? Then, so should we be good Samaritans, as if we were commissioned by Jesus Christ Himself, to all those who are in need of our help. So start today to do good and to be good to others. You will be blessed in your efforts.

In Summary

Now that you have read through all the preceding text, I assume that your knowledge concerning the Twelve Commandments has grown considerably. Hopefully your appreciation and love for Father in Heaven and His son Jesus Christ has greatly increased and that you have grown considerably closer to Them. It is hoped that you are well on your way to becoming a godly person in your personal behavior. If so, my intent in writing the book is thus satisfied.

I appreciate the fact that you have endeavored to read the entire text, and also, possibly the companion workbook. Whether you purchased the book yourself or had it given to you, I remain thankful for the purchase. If you have made it this far, I am even more thankful that you have endeavored to read, study and implement many of the ideas, thoughts, suggestions and directives into your everyday life. You will be thankful too, if you are not already so.

In summary, I originally intended to write a book that not only would accomplish my intent, but also give the reader some memory aids or mnemonics concerning the Twelve Commandments that go beyond the completed worksheets and charts in the workbook. Deeply embedded in the Data Analysis section in the workbook is a discussion on the four main areas of interest which inspired the research, which gave birth to this book. They are: ***1)*** determine how well people can remember the Twelve Commandments, ***2)*** determine how well people can properly order the Twelve Commandments, ***3)*** determine if people know what the meaning of each commandment is, and *4)* determine if gender, age, or whether the respondent is an active Christian, would have any effect upon the responses to the above four areas of interest.

With the exception of the majority of those who were active in some Christian church, the data showed that most people did not know more than three or four of the commandments. The data on the meaning of each commandment was even less encouraging. If you are interested in such things, you are encouraged to read the Data Analysis section in the workbook for greater detail. Suffice it to say, people today do not know the basic commandments very well.

However, in discussing the order of the commandments, which I originally did not think was important, there is some interesting information that I want to now impart to you. It became apparent to me that the order of the commandments was intentional and thus, very important.

There are three main groupings within the Ten Commandments. They begin with the first group of three commandments which address our most important relationship with our savior Jesus Christ, the Jehovah and God of the Old Testament, the Creator under direction of our Holy Father in Heaven. It is only appropriate that these three commandments are first, since Jesus is the Creator and God of this earth. The next two commandments of keeping the Sabbath day holy and honoring our earthly father and mother are not quite as mighty as the first three where we are commanded to honor Jehovah or God. However, these two commandments are very important and are more lofty and higher commandments than the next five short "Thou shalt not" commandments. If we are living the first five commandments, then we will likely be living in harmony with all the short "Thou shalt not" commandments. The last five commandments are the basic behavioral commandments.

Remembering the order of the Ten Commandments is an easy task if one puts his or her mind to the task for only a few minutes. For instance, as stated above, the first three deal with our relationship with Jehovah, God of the Old Testament and I believe with also the holy Father, the God of us all. The first commandment is that we are not to have any other gods before God the Father, or God Jehovah. The second, is that we are not to worship or have any graven images or idols of God or Jehovah, or anything else, and the third is to not take their names in vain.

The first group of commandments can be easily remembered with the following mnemonic, or memory aid. Remember, that "<u>One God has no Graven, Vains.</u>" It is recognized by the author that those things which transport blood back to the heart, are called veins, not vains. However, you should also remember that mnemonics are not necessarily always accurate either in content or in making sense, they are only aids in remembering things. And, as is often the case, the more nonsensical a mnemonic is, usually the easier it is to remember.

The second group of commandments have to do with keeping the Sabbath day holy and honoring your earthly father and mother. Just remember, "<u>On the Sabbath day, Honor parents.</u>"

The third grouping consists of the five short "Thou shalt not" commandments. Remember this mnemonic as though you were in Old Testament times. Thus, "<u>Kill all those Adulterous Stealers, who Lie and Covet.</u>" Or better, if you prefer New Testament times, you would remember to "Don't Kill, even those Adulterous Stealers, who Lie and Covet."

Thus, in review:

"One God, has no Graven Vains."
"On the Sabbath day, Honor Parents."
"Don't Kill, even those Adulterous,
Stealers who Lie and Covet."

The Two Great Commandments, are considered separately, since they are commandments that came from the Savior Himself in the New Testament. They are easy to remember in that we are to first "Love God with all our Heart, Soul, Mind and Strength," and then to "Love thy Neighbor as Thyself."

Thus, in review:

"Love God Greatly."
"Love your Neighbor as Yourself."

In summary, as Jesus Christ indicated when giving the Two Great Commandments in Matthew 22:34-40, in Mark 12:28-34, and in Luke 10:25-37, "On these two commandments hang all the law and the prophets." It is most likely that when a person is living the Two Great Commandments he or she will also be living in harmony with all the other commandments, including the original Ten Commandments.

Any devout Jewish person taking the Quiz or the Questionnaire in the workbook, would be expected to know much about the Ten Commandments and their proper order and meaning as given in Exodus. However, he or she would not be expected to unfortunately know much about the Two Great Commandments given by Jesus Christ. And therein is a great shame, for the devout Jews of today are still suffering from the sins of their forefathers, and will continue to do so until Jesus Christ returns again in His triumphant and glorious second coming.

The Jews will someday know that Jesus was the Jehovah of the Old Testament and is, in fact, the very Christ, the Messiah, the Savior, the Redeemer of the world, the literal son of God. He really has indeed already come, and will yet come a second time "...in the name of the Lord." As surely as both the Old and New Testaments testify, and other more modern-day scriptures testify of the great event to come, He will return. His name was and is Jesus Christ, the very Son of God the Eternal Father, who is the spiritual Father of us all.

When one can evidence that he or she knows the order of the Ten Commandments, as well as provide knowledge of the Two Great Commandments, he or she has indeed studied the commandments. But studying the commandments does not necessarily mean one is keeping the commandments, which should be the goal of every person.

Now that you know the commandments from your reading and studying, it is my sincere hope that you will keep all twelve of the commandments to the very best of your ability for the rest of your life. If you are not entirely successful from time to time, then try harder the next time to really change your behavior. Remember that repentance should be an integral part of your everyday life, but do not repeat your mistakes. Learn from your repented mistakes. Don't repeat them. ***Keep going onward and upward in your quest for personal righteous behavior.***

May God the Father through His precious son Jesus Christ, grant unto you quiet resolve to succeed. May the Holy Ghost through his wonderful power and testimony be your guide and give you a testimony that Jesus Christ is indeed the Savior of mankind. Seek to be baptized by one who has the proper authority, then go forth to be an example and a minister of goodness and truth for the rest of your life. You will be greatly blessed. May God our Heavenly Father bless you in your efforts to be more like Him.

Acknowedgments

The author would like to thank several people for significantly contributing to the completion of this book. To Brenda Smyth for her spiritual nature, great faith and quiet example. To Scott Sargent for his inspirational cover design, formatting and publication suggestions. To Scott's parents, Sheldon and Deana Sargent, for their friendship over the years and their helpful suggestions. To Dr. Beatrice Mathews Sparks for her encouragement and suggestions. To Blain Hudson for his editing strokes and uplifting comments. To Mr. John Giberson for his insightful critique. To the wonderful but unknown donor of $1,000 to help print the book.

To Hyrum and Gail Smith for their suggestions to add Case Studies to the book, which helped considerably. To my parents, Harley and Marie Endsley, for their good examples of living the commandments. To my brothers, David and Ray and my sister Carolyn for their good examples, help and friendship to me. To my first wife Marsha, who died in November of 1995, for her great examples of honesty and integrity which she displayed throughout her life. To my special and talented daughter Amanda Marie Endsley for her scripture proofing and comments. To my spiritual step-daughter Jennifer Feller Davis for her scripture proofing. To my super sister-in-law Carolyn Robertson for her excitement, support and suggestions. A special thanks to Carolyn Chamberlain for her insightful comments, suggestions and critique which significantly improved the book. To grandma Ranta for her support and encouragement. To my new wife Nancy and her other children of Ben, Rebecca, Erin, Kathy, Doug and Barbara for their quiet encouragement. To my other children of Tyler, Adam, Logan and Mariah for their support, tolerance and just being super kids. And now especially to my wife Nancy. Her encouragement and economic support while I was writing enabled me to complete the book with a minimum of down-time. Without her support the book would not have been written.

And finally, the author publicaly expresses his grateful appreciation to Heavenly Father, to His son Jesus Christ, and to the Holy Ghost for providing the inspiration and knowledge to write, and the patience to complete the book. There have been many obstacles which have been overcome and they have been overcome principally due to Their help.

In advance, a special thanks to those of you who have purchased the book and or the workbook, either for yourself or for someone else to read. May you receive great blessings from reading them, for completing the activities in the workbook, or for putting the suggestions into your everyday life. Or giving either of them to someone so that he or she can improve their own life by their better understanding, and then living the commandments with greater fidelity.

I can be reached at the following email address if you wish to share comments or correspond with me about the topics addressed in the book: **wendsley@sginet.com**